The World Is At Your Command

The Very Best of Neville Goddard

A Compilation of Neville's Best Chapters/Teachings

Edited and Compiled
by
David Allen

Copyright © 2017

Copyright © 2017 by Shanon Allen / David Allen

All rights reserved. No part of this publication may be reproduced, distributed, or transmitted in any form or by any means, including photocopying, recording, or other electronic or mechanical methods, without the prior written permission of the publisher, except in the case of brief quotations embodied in critical reviews and certain other noncommercial uses permitted by copyright law. Printed in the United States of America.

First Printing, December 2017

ISBN: 978-0-9995435-0-4

Visit Us At **NevilleGoddardBooks.com** for a complete listing of all our books and **1000's of Free Books to Read online and download.**

The Chapters:

Chapter	Page	Title
Chapter 1 -	7	You Shall Decree
Chapter 2 -	11	To Him Who Hath
Chapter 3 -	14	The Twelve Disciples
Chapter 4 -	23	The Name of God
Chapter 5 -	27	The Law of Creation
Chapter 6 -	30	The Secret of Feeling
Chapter 7 -	38	Desire, The Word of God
Chapter 8 -	44	Law of Reversibility
Chapter 9 -	47	Imagination and Faith
Chapter 10 -	52	Power of Imagination
Chapter 11 -	58	No One to Change But Self
Chapter 12 -	62	Law and its Operation
Chapter 13 -	69	Spirit – Feeling
Chapter 14 -	71	I AM
Chapter 15 -	74	Consciousness
Chapter 16 -	77	Power of Assumption
Chapter 17 -	81	Desire
Chapter 18 -	83	The Truth That Sets You Free
Chapter 19 -	86	Creation
Chapter 20 -	88	All Things Are Possible
Chapter 21 -	90	Who is Your Imagination?
Chapter 22 -	98	Highways of the Inner World
Chapter 23 -	104	The Pruning Shears of Revision
Chapter 24 -	111	The Coin of Heaven
Chapter 25 -	121	It is Within
Chapter 26 -	126	"The Law" Imagining Creates Reality
Chapter 27 -	134	There is no Fiction
Chapter 28 -	145	The Creative Moment

Foreword

The chapters I have chosen for this compilation (28 in all) are simply the those that have made the most impact on transforming my life. Are they the very best of Neville? They are to me. I will let the reader decide for themselves if they are to them as well.

David Allen

Metaphysical / Law of Attraction Books

David Allen - The Power of I AM (2014), The Power of I AM - Volume 2 (2015), The Power of I AM - Volume 3 (2017)

David Allen - The Creative Power of Thought, Man's Greatest Discovery (2017)

David Allen - The Secrets, Mysteries & Powers of The Subconscious Mind (2017)

David Allen - The Money Bible - The Secrets of Attracting Prosperity (2017)

David Allen - Your Faith Is Your Fortune, Your Unlimited Power

The Neville Goddard Collection (All 10 of his books plus 2 Lecture series) (2016)

Neville Goddard - Assumptions Harden Into Facts: The Book (2016)

Neville Goddard - Imagination: The Redemptive Power in Man (2016)

Neville Goddard - The World is At Your Command - The Very Best of Neville Goddard (2017)

Neville Goddard - Imagining Creates Reality - 365 Mystical Daily Quotes (2017)

Neville Goddard's Interpretation of Scripture (2018)

The Definitive Christian D. Larson Collection (6 Volumes, 30 books) (2014)

The World Is At Your Command

Chapter 1

Chapter 2 of Your Faith is Your Fortune

You Shall Decree

*"So shall My word be that goeth forth out of
My mouth; it shall not return unto Me void,
but it shall accomplish that which I please,
and it shall prosper in the thing whereto I sent it."*

Man can decree a thing and it will come to pass.

Man has always decreed that which has appeared in his world. He is today decreeing that which is appearing in his world and he shall continue to do so as long as man is conscious of being man.

Nothing has ever appeared in man's world, but what man decreed that it should. This you may deny; but try as you will, you cannot disprove it for this decreeing is based upon a changeless principle.

Man does not command things to appear by his words, which are, more often than not, a confession of his doubts and fears.

Decreeing is ever done in consciousness.

Every man automatically expresses that which he is conscious of being. Without effort or the use of words, at every moment of time, man is commanding himself to be and to possess that which he is conscious of being and possessing.

This changeless principle of expression is dramatized in all the Bibles of the world.

The writers of our sacred books were illumined mystics, past masters in the art of psychology. In telling the story of the soul, they personified this impersonal principle in the form of a historical document both to preserve it and to hide it from the eyes of the uninitiated.

Today, those to whom this great treasure has been entrusted, namely, the priesthoods of the world, have forgotten that the Bibles are psychological dramas representing the consciousness of man; in their blind forgetfulness, they now teach their followers to worship its characters as men and women who actually lived in time and space.

When man sees the Bible as a great psychological drama, with all of its characters and actors as the personified qualities and attributes of his own consciousness, then and then only will the Bible reveal to him the light of its symbology.

This Impersonal principle of life which made all things is personified as God. This Lord God, creator of heaven and earth, is discovered to be man's awareness of being.

If man were less bound by orthodoxy and more intuitively observant, he could not fail to notice in the reading of the Bibles that the awareness of being is revealed hundreds of times throughout this literature.

To name a few:

"I AM hath sent me unto you."

"Be still and know that I AM God."

"I AM the Lord and there is no God."

"I AM the shepherd."

"I AM the door."

"I AM the resurrection and the life."

"I AM the way."

"I AM the beginning and the end."

I AM; man's unconditioned awareness of being is revealed as Lord and Creator of every conditioned state of being.

If man would give up his belief in a God apart from himself, recognize his awareness of being to be God (this awareness fashions itself in the likeness and image of its conception of itself), he would transform his world from a barren waste to a fertile field of his own liking.

The day man does this he will know that he and his Father are one, but his Father is greater than he.

He will know that his consciousness of being is one with that which he is conscious of being, but that his unconditioned consciousness of being is greater than his conditioned state or his conception of himself.

When man discovers his consciousness to be the impersonal power of expression, which power eternally personifies itself in his conceptions of himself, he will assume and appropriate that state of consciousness which he desires to express; in so doing he will become that state in expression.

"Ye shall decree a thing and it shall come to pass"

can now be told in this manner:

You shall become conscious of being or possessing a thing and you shall express or possess that which you are conscious of being.

The law of consciousness is the only law of expression.

"I AM the way".

"I AM the resurrection".

Consciousness is the way as well as the power which resurrects and expresses all that man will ever be conscious of being.

Turn from the blindness of the uninitiated man who attempts to express and possess those qualities and things which he is not conscious of being and possessing; and be as the illumined mystic who decrees, on the basis of this changeless law.

Consciously claim yourself to be that which you seek; appropriate the consciousness of that which you see; and you too will know the status of the true mystic, as follows:

I became conscious of being it. I am still conscious of being it. And I shall continue to be conscious of being it until that which I am conscious of being is perfectly expressed.

"Yes, I shall decree a thing and it shall come to pass."

Chapter 2

Chapter 10 of Your Faith is Your Fortune

To Him Who Hath

"Take heed therefore how ye hear;
for whosoever hath, to him shall be
given; and whosoever hath not, from
him shall be taken even that which he
seemeth to have."

The Bible, which is the greatest psychological book ever written, warns man to be aware of what he hears; then follows this warning with the statement,

"To him that hath it shall be given
and to him that hath not it shall be taken away".

Though many look upon this statement as one of the most cruel and unjust of the sayings attributed to Jesus, it still remains a just and merciful law based upon life's changeless principle of expression.

Man's ignorance of the working of the law does not excuse him nor save him from the results.

Law is impersonal and therefore no respecter of persons. Man is warned to be selective in that which he hears and accepts as true. Everything that man accepts as true leaves an impression on his consciousness and must in time be defined as proof or disproof.

Perceptive hearing is the perfect medium through which man registers impressions. A man must discipline himself to hear only that which he wants to hear, regardless of rumors or the evidence of his senses to the contrary.

As he conditions his perceptive hearing, he will react only to those impressions which he has decided upon. This law never fails. Fully conditioned, man becomes incapable of hearing other than that which contributes to his desire.

God, as you have discovered, is that unconditioned awareness which gives to you all that you are aware of being.

To be aware of being or having anything is to be or have that which you are aware of being.

Upon this changeless principle all things rest. It is impossible for anything to be other than that which it is aware of being.

"To him that hath (that which he is aware of being) it shall be given".

Good, bad or indifferent, it does not matter, man receives multiplied a hundredfold that which he is aware of being.

In keeping with this changeless law,

"To him that hath not, it shall be taken from him and added to the one that hath",

the rich get richer and the poor get poorer. You can only magnify that which you are conscious of being.

All things gravitate to that consciousness with which they are in tune.

Likewise, all things disentangle themselves from that consciousness with which they are out of tune.

Divide the wealth of the world equally among all men and in a short time, this equal division will be as originally disproportioned. Wealth will find its way back into the pockets of those from whom it was taken.

Instead of joining the chorus of the have-nots who insist on destroying those who have, recognize this changeless law of expression.

Consciously define yourself as that which you desire.

Once defined, your conscious claim established, continue in this confidence until the reward is received.

As surely as the day follows the night, any attribute, consciously claimed, will manifest itself.

Thus, that which to the sleeping orthodox world is a cruel and unjust law becomes to the enlightened one of the most merciful and just statements of truth.

"I AM come not to destroy but to fulfill."

Nothing is actually destroyed. Any seeming destruction is a result of a change in consciousness.

Consciousness ever fills full the state in which it dwells.

The state from which consciousness is detached seems to those not familiar with this law to be destructive.

However, this is only preparatory to a new state of consciousness.

Claim yourself to be that which you want filled full.

"Nothing is destroyed. All is fulfilled."

"To him that hath it shall be given"

Chapter 3

Chapter 18 of Your Faith is Your Fortune

The Twelve Disciples

> *"And when He had called unto Him His twelve disciples, He gave them power against unclean spirits, to cast them out, and to heal all manner of sickness and all manner of disease."*

The twelve disciples represent the twelve qualities of mind, which can be controlled and disciplined by man. If disciplined, they will at all times, obey the command, of the one who has disciplined them.

These twelve qualities in man are potentials of every mind. Undisciplined, their actions resemble more the actions of a mob than they do of a trained and disciplined army. All the storms and confusions that engulf man can be traced directly to these twelve ill-related characteristics of the human mind in its present slumbering state.

Until they are awakened and disciplined, they will permit every rumor and sensuous emotion to move them.

When these twelve are disciplined and brought under control, the one who accomplishes this control will say to them,

> *"Hereafter I call you not slaves, but friends"*

He knows that from that moment on, each acquired disciplined attribute of mind will befriend and protect him.

The names of the twelve qualities reveal their natures. These names are not given to them until they are called to discipleship.

They are: Simon, who was later surnamed Peter, Andrew, James, John, Philip, Bartholomew, Thomas, Matthew, James the son of Alphaeus, Thaddaeus, Simon the Canaanite and Judas.

1st DISCIPLE OR QUALITY OF MIND
Simon

The first quality to be called and disciplined is Simon, or the attribute of hearing. This faculty, when lifted to the level of a disciple, permits only such impressions to reach consciousness as those which his hearing has commanded him to let enter. No matter what the wisdom of man might suggest or the evidence of his senses convey, if such suggestions and ideas are not in keeping with that which he hears, he remains unmoved.

This one has been instructed by his Lord and made to understand that every suggestion he permits to pass his gate will, on reaching his Lord and Master (his consciousness), leave its impression there, which impression must in time become an expression.

The instruction to Simon is that he should permit only dignified and honorable visitors or impressions to enter the house (consciousness) of his Lord. No mistake can be covered up or hidden from his Master, for every expression of life tells his Lord whom he consciously or unconsciously entertained.

When Simon, by his works, proves himself to be a true and faithful disciple, then he receives the surname of Peter, or the rock, the unmoved disciple, the one who cannot be bribed or coerced by any visitor. He is called by his Lord Simon Peter, the one who faithfully hears the commands of his Lord and besides which commands he hears not.

It is this Simon Peter who discovers the I AM to be Christ, and for his discovery is given the keys to heaven, and is made the foundation stone upon which the Temple of God rests. Buildings must have firm foundations and only the disciplined hearing can, on learning that the I AM is Christ, remain firm and unmoved in the knowledge that I AM Christ and beside ME there is no savior.

2nd DISCIPLE OR QUALITY OF MIND
Andrew

The second quality to be called to discipleship is Andrew, or courage. As the first quality, faith in oneself, is developed, it automatically calls into being its brother, courage. Faith in oneself, which asks no man's help but quietly and alone appropriates the consciousness of the quality desired and . . in spite of reason or the evidence of his senses to the contrary continues faithful-patiently waiting in the knowledge that his unseen claim if sustained must be realized . . such faith develops a courage and strength of character that are beyond the wildest dreams of the undisciplined man whose faith is in things seen.

The faith of the undisciplined man cannot really be called faith. For if the armies, medicines or wisdom of man in which his faith is placed be taken from him, his faith and courage go with it. But from the disciplined one the whole world could be taken and yet he would remain faithful in the knowledge that the state of consciousness in which he abides must in due season embody itself. This courage is Peter's brother Andrew, the disciple, who knows what it is to dare, to do and to be silent.

3rd and 4th DISCIPLES OR QUALITIES OF MIND
James and John

The next two (third & fourth) who are called are also related. These are the brothers, James and John, James the just, the righteous judge, and his brother John, the beloved. Justice to be wise must be administered with love, ever turning the other cheek and at all times returning good for evil, love for hate, non-violence for violence.

The disciple James, symbol of a disciplined judgment, must, when raised to the high office of a supreme judge, be blindfolded that he may not be influenced by the flesh nor judge after the appearances of being. Disciplined judgment is administered by one who is not influenced by appearances. The one who has called these brothers to discipleship continues faithful to his command to hear only that which he has been commanded to hear, namely, the Good. The man who has this quality of his mind disciplined is incapable of hearing and accepting as true anything, either of himself or another, which does not on the hearing, fill his heart with love.

These two disciples or aspects of the mind are one and inseparable when awakened. Such a disciplined one forgives all men for being that which they are. He knows as a wise judge that every man perfectly expresses that which he is, as man, conscious of being. He knows that upon the changeless foundation of consciousness all manifestation rests, that changes of expression can be brought about only through changes of consciousness.

With neither condemnation nor criticism, these disciplined qualities of the mind permit everyone to be that which he is. However, although allowing this perfect freedom of choice to all, they are nevertheless ever watchful to see that they themselves prophesy and do . . both for others and themselves . . only such things which when expressed glorify, dignify and give joy to the expresser.

5th DISCIPLE OR QUALITY OF MIND
Philip

The fifth quality called to discipleship is Philip. This one asked to be shown the Father. The awakened man knows that the Father is the state of consciousness in which man dwells, and that this state or Father can be seen only as it is expressed. He knows himself to be the perfect likeness or image of that consciousness with which he is identified. So He declares,

> "No man has at any time seen My Father; but I, the Son, who dwelleth in His bosom have revealed Him; therefore, when you see Me, the Son, you see My Father, for I come to bear witness of My Father"

I and My Father, consciousness and its expression, God and man, are one.

This aspect of the mind, when disciplined, persists until ideas, ambitions and desires become embodied realities. This is the quality which states

"Yet in my flesh shall I see God."

It knows how to make the word flesh, how to give form to the formless.

6th DISCIPLE OR QUALITY OF MIND
Bartholomew

The sixth disciple is called Bartholomew. This quality is the imaginative faculty, which quality of the mind when once awake distinguishes one from the masses. An awakened imagination places the one so awakened head and shoulders above the average man, giving him the appearance of a beacon light in a world of darkness. No quality so separates man from man as does the disciplined imagination. This is the separation of the wheat from the chaff. Those who have given most to Society are our artists, scientists, inventors and others with vivid imaginations.

Should a survey be made to determine the reason why so many seemingly educated men and women fail in their after-college years or should it be made to determine the reason for the different earning powers of the masses, there would be no doubt but that imagination played the important part. Such a survey would show that it is imagination which makes one a leader while the lack of it makes one a follower.

Instead of developing the imagination of man, our educational system oftentimes stifles it by attempting to put into the mind of man the wisdom he seeks. It forces him to memorize a number of text books which, all too soon, are disproved by later text books. Education is not accomplished by putting something into man; its purpose is to draw out of man the wisdom which is latent within him. May the reader call Bartholomew to discipleship, for only as this quality is raised to discipleship will you have the capacity to conceive ideas that will lift you beyond the limitations of man.

7th DISCIPLE OR QUALITY OF MIND
Thomas

The seventh is called Thomas. This disciplined quality doubts or denies every rumor and suggestion that are not in harmony with that which Simon Peter has been commanded to let enter. The man who is conscious of being healthy (not because of inherited health, diets or climate, but because he is awakened and knows the state of consciousness in which he lives) will, in spite of the conditions of the world, continue to express health.

He could hear, through the press, radio and wise men of the world that a plague was sweeping the earth and yet he would remain unmoved and unimpressed. Thomas, the doubter, when disciplined, would deny that sickness or anything else which was not in sympathy with the consciousness to which he belonged had any power to affect him.

This quality of denial, when disciplined, protects man from receiving impressions that are not in harmony with his nature. He adopts an attitude of total indifference to all suggestions that are foreign to that which he desires to express. Disciplined denial is not a fight or a struggle but total indifference.

8th DISCIPLE OR QUALITY OF MIND
Matthew

Matthew, the eighth, is the gift of God. This quality of the mind reveals man's desires as gifts of God. The man who has called this disciple into being knows that every desire of his heart is a gift from heaven and that it contains both the power and the plan of its self-expression.

Such a man never questions the manner of its expression. He knows that the plan of expression is never revealed to man for God's ways are past finding out. He fully accepts his desires as gifts already received and goes his way in peace confident that they shall appear.

9th DISCIPLE OR QUALITY OF MIND
James

The ninth disciple is called James, the son of Alphaeus. This is the quality of discernment. A clear and ordered mind is the voice which calls this disciple into being. This faculty perceives that which is not revealed to the eye of man. This disciple judges not from appearances for it has the capacity to function in the realm of causes and so is never misled by appearances.

Clairvoyance is the faculty which is awakened when this quality is developed and disciplined, not the clairvoyance of the mediumistic séance rooms, but the true clairvoyance or clear seeing of the mystic. That is, this aspect of the mind has the capacity to interpret that which is seen. Discernment or the capacity to diagnose is the quality of James the son of Alphaeus.

10th DISCIPLE OR QUALITY OF MIND
Thaddaeus

Thaddaeus, the tenth, is the disciple of praise, a quality in which the undisciplined man is woefully lacking. When this quality of praise and thanksgiving is awake within man, he walks with the words, "Thank you, Father", ever on his lips.

He knows that his thanks for things not seen opens the windows of heaven and permits gifts beyond his capacity to receive to be poured upon him.

The man who is not thankful for things received is not likely to be the recipient of many gifts from the same source. Until this quality of the mind is disciplined, man will not see the desert blossom as the rose. Praise and thanksgiving are to the invisible gifts of God (one's desires) what rain and sun are to the unseen seeds in the bosom of the earth.

11th DISCIPLE OR QUALITY OF MIND
Simon of Canaan

The eleventh quality called is Simon of Canaan. A good key phrase for this disciple is "Hearing good news".

Simon of Canaan, or Simon from the land of milk and honey, when called to discipleship, is proof that the one who calls this faculty into being has become conscious of the abundant life. He can say with the Psalmist David,

> *"Thou preparest a table before me in the presence of mine enemies; thou anointest my head with oil; my cup runneth over."*

This disciplined aspect of the mind is incapable of hearing anything other than good news and so is well qualified to preach the Gospel or Good-spell.

12th DISCIPLE OR QUALITY OF MIND
Judas

The twelfth and last of the disciplined qualities of the mind is called Judas.

When this quality is awake, man knows that he must die to that which he is before he can become that which he desires to be. So it is said of this disciple that he committed suicide, which is the mystic's way of telling the initiated, that Judas is the disciplined aspect of detachment. This one knows that his I AM or consciousness is his savior, so he lets all other saviors go. This quality, when disciplined, gives one the strength to let go.

The man who has called Judas into being has learned how to take his attention away from problems or limitations and to place it upon that which is the solution or savior.

> *"Except ye be born again, you cannot in anywise enter the Kingdom of Heaven."*

> *"No greater love hath man than this, that he give his life for a friend"*

When man realizes that the quality desired, if realized, would save and befriend him, he willingly gives up his life (present conception of himself) for his friend by detaching his consciousness from that which he is conscious of being and assuming the consciousness of that which he desires to be.

Judas, the one whom the world in its ignorance has blackened, will, when man awakes from his undisciplined state, be placed on high for God is love and no greater love has a man than this . . that he lay down his life for a friend. Until man lets go of that which he is now conscious of being, he will not become that which he desires to be; and Judas is the one who accomplishes this through suicide or detachment.

These are the twelve qualities which were given to man in the foundation of the world. Man's duty is to raise them to the level of discipleship. When this is accomplished, man will say,

*"I have finished the work which thou gavest Me to do.
I have glorified Thee on earth and now,
O, Father, glorify Thou Me with Thine
own Self with the glory which I had
with Thee before the world was."*

Chapter 4

Chapter 2 of Freedom for All

The Name of God

It cannot be stated too often that consciousness is the one and only reality, for this is the truth that sets man free.

This is the foundation upon which the whole structure of biblical literature rests. The stories of the Bible are all mystical revelations written in an Eastern symbolism which reveals to the intuitive the secret of creation and the formula of escape.

The Bible is man's attempt to express in words the cause and manner of creation.

Man discovered that his consciousness was the cause or creator of his world, so he proceeded to tell the story of creation in a series of symbolical stories known to us today as the Bible.

To understand this greatest of books you need a little intelligence and much intuition . . intelligence enough to enable you to read the book, and intuition enough to interpret and understand what you read.

You may ask why the Bible was written symbolically. Why was it not written in a clear, simple style so that all who read it might understand it? To these questions I reply that all men speak symbolically to that part of the world which differs from their own.

The language of the West is clear to us of the West, but it is symbolic to the East; and vice versa. An example of this can be found in the Easterner's instruction:

"If thine hand offend thee, cut it off."

He speaks of the hand, not as the hand of the body, but as any form of expression, and thereby he warns you to turn from that expression in your world which is offensive to you.

At the same time the man of the West would unintentionally mislead the man of the East by saying:

"This bank is on the rocks."

For the expression

"on the rocks"

to the Westerner is equivalent to bankruptcy while a rock to an Easterner is a symbol of faith and security.

"I will like him unto a wise man which built his house upon a rock; and the rain descended, and the floods came, and the winds blew and beat upon that house; and it fell not; for it was founded upon a rock."

To really understand the message of the Bible you must bear in mind that it was written by the Eastern mind and therefore cannot be taken literally by those of the West.

Biologically, there is no difference between the East and the West. Love and hate are the same; hunger and thirst are the same; ambition and desire are the same; but the technique of expression is vastly different.

The first thing you must discover if you would unlock the secret of the Bible, is the meaning of the symbolic name of the creator which is known to all as Jehovah.

This word "Jehovah" is composed of the four Hebrew letters . . JOD HE VAU HE. The whole secret of creation is concealed within this name.

The first letter, JOD, represents the absolute state or consciousness unconditioned; the sense of undefined awareness; that all-inclusiveness out of which all creation or conditioned states of consciousness come. In the terminology of today JOD is I AM, or unconditioned consciousness.

The second letter, HE, represents the only begotten Son, a desire, an imaginary state. It symbolizes an idea; a defined subjective state or clarified mental picture.

The third letter, VAU, symbolizes the act of unifying or joining the conceiver (JOD), the consciousness desiring to the conception (HE), the state desired, so that the conceiver and the conception become one. Fixing a mental state, consciously defining yourself as the state desired, impressing upon yourself the fact that you are now that which you imagined or conceived as your objective, is the function of VAU.

It nails or joins the consciousness desiring to the thing desired. The cementing or joining process is accomplished subjectively by feeling the reality of that which is not yet objectified.

The fourth letter, HE, represents the objectifying of this subjective agreement. The JOD HE VAU makes man or the manifested world (HE), in the image and likeness of itself, the subjective conscious state. So the function of the final HE is to objectively bear witness to the subjective state JOD HE VAU. Conditioned consciousness continually objectifies itself on the screen of space. The world is the image and likeness of the subjective conscious state which created it. The visible world of itself can do nothing; it only bears record of its creator, the subjective state. It is the visible Son (HE) bearing witness of the invisible Father, Son and Mother . . JOD HE VAU . . a Holy Trinity which can only be seen when made visible as man or manifestation.

Your unconditioned consciousness (JOD) is your I AM which visualizes or imagines a desirable state (HE), and then becomes conscious of being that state imagined by feeling and believing itself to be the imagined state. The conscious union between you who desire and that which you desire to be, is made possible through the VAU, or your capacity to feel and believe.

Believing is simply living in the feeling of actually being the state imagined, by assuming the consciousness of being the state desired. The subjective state symbolized as JOD HE VAU then objectifies itself as HE, thereby completing the mystery of the creator's name and nature, JOD HE VAU HE (Jehovah). JOD is to be aware; HE is to be aware of something; VAU is to be aware as, or to be aware of being that which you were only aware of. The second HE is your visible objectified world which is made in the image and likeness of the JOD HE VAU, or that which you are aware of being.

> "And God said, Let Us make man in
> Our image, after Our likeness."

Let us, JOD HE VAU make the objective manifestation (HE) in our image, the image of the subjective state. The world is the objectified likeness of the subjective conscious state in which consciousness abides.

This understanding that consciousness is the one and only reality is the foundation of the Bible.

The stories of the Bible are attempts to reveal in symbolic language the secret of creation as well as to show man the one formula to escape from all of his own creations.

This is the true meaning of the name of Jehovah, the name by which all things are made and without which there is nothing made that is made.

First, you are aware; then you become aware of something; then you become aware as that which you were aware of; then you behold objectively that which you are aware of being.

Chapter 5

Chapter 3 of Freedom for All

The Law of Creation

Let us take one of the stories of the Bible and see how the prophets and writers of old revealed the story of creation by this strange Eastern symbolism.

We all know the story of Noah and the Ark; that Noah was chosen to create a new world after the world was destroyed by the flood.

The Bible tells us that Noah had three sons, Shem, Ham and Japheth.

The first son is called Shem, which means name. Ham. The second son, means warm, alive. The third son is called Japheth, which means extension.

You will observe that Noah and his three sons Shem, Ham and Japheth contain the same formula of creation as does the divine name of JOD HE VAU HE.

Noah, the Father, the conceiver, the builder of a new world is equivalent to the JOD, or unconditioned consciousness, I AM.

Shem is your desire; that which you are conscious of; that which you name and define as your objective, and is equivalent to the second letter in the divine name (HE).

Ham is the warm, live state of feeling, which joins or binds together consciousness desiring and the thing desired, and is therefore equivalent to the third letter in the divine name, the VAU.

The last son, Japheth, means extension, and is the extended or objectified state bearing witness of the subjective state and is equivalent to the last letter in the divine name, HE.

You are Noah, the knower, the creator. The first thing you beget is an idea, an urge, a desire, the word, or your first son Shem (name).

Your second son Ham (warm, alive) is the secret of feeling by which you are joined to your desire subjectively so that you, the consciousness desiring, become conscious of being or possessing the thing desired.

Your third son, Japheth, is the confirmation, the visible proof that you know the secret of creation. He is the extended or objectified state bearing witness of the invisible or subjective state in which you abide.

In the story of Noah it is recorded that Ham saw the secrets of his Father, and because of his discovery, he was made to serve his brothers, Shem and Japheth.

Ham, or feeling, is the secret of the Father, your I AM, for it is through feeling that the consciousness desiring is joined to the thing desired. The conscious union or mystical marriage is made possible only through feeling. It is feeling which performs this heavenly union of Father and Son,

Noah and Shem, unconditioned consciousness and conditioned consciousness. By performing this service, feeling automatically serves Japheth, the extended or expressed state, for there can be no objectified expression unless there is first a subjective impression.

To feel the presence of the thing desired, to subjectively actualize a state by impressing upon yourself, through feeling, a definite conscious state is the secret of creation.

Your present objectified world is Japheth which was made visible by Ham. Therefore Ham serves his brothers Shem and Japheth, for without feeling which is symbolized as Ham, the idea or thing desired (Shem) could not be made visible as Japheth.

The ability to feel the unseen, the ability to actualize and make real a definite subjective state through the sense of feeling is the secret of creation, the secret by which the word or unseen desire is made visible . . is made flesh.

> *"And God calleth things that be*
> *not as though they were."*

Consciousness calls things that are not seen as though they were, and it does this by first defining itself as that which it desires to express, and second by remaining within the defined state until the invisible becomes visible. Here is the perfect working of the law according to the story of Noah. This very moment you are aware of being.

This awareness of being, this knowing that you are, is Noah, the creator.

Now with Noah's identity established as your own consciousness of being, name something that you would like to possess or express; define some objective (Shem), and with your desire clearly defined, close your eyes and feel that you have it or are expressing it.

Don't question how it can be done; simply feel that you have it. Assume the attitude of mind that would be yours if you were already in possession of it so that you feel that it is done.

Feeling is the secret of creation.

Be as wise as Ham and make this discovery that you too may have the joy of serving your brothers Shem and Japheth; the joy of making the word or name flesh.

Chapter 6

Chapter 4 of Freedom for All

The Secret of Feeling

The secret of feeling or the calling of the invisible into visible states is beautifully told in the story of Isaac blessing his second son Jacob by the belief, based solely upon feeling, that he was blessing his first son Esau.

It is recorded that Isaac, who was old and blind, felt that he was about to leave this world and wishing to bless his first son Esau before he died, sent Esau hunting for savory venison with the promise that upon his return from the hunt he would receive his father's blessing.

Now Jacob, who desired the birthright or right to be born through the blessing of his father, overheard his blind father's request for venison and his promise to Esau. So, as Esau went hunting for the venison, Jacob killed and dressed a kid of his father's flock.

Placing the skins upon his smooth body to give him the feel of his hairy and rough brother Esau, he brought the tastily prepared kid to his blind father Isaac. And Isaac who depended solely upon his sense of feel mistook his second son Jacob for his first son Esau, and pronounced his blessing on Jacob.

Esau on his return from the hunt learned that his smooth-skinned brother Jacob had supplanted him so he appealed to his father for justice; but Isaac answered and said,

"Thy brother came with subtlety and hath taken away thy blessing.

I have made him thy Lord, and all his brethren have I given to him for servants."

Simple human decency should tell man that this story cannot be taken literally.

There must be a message for man hidden somewhere in this treacherous and despicable act of Jacob!

The hidden message, the formula of success buried in this story was intuitively revealed to the writer in this manner:

Isaac, the blind father, is your consciousness; your awareness of being.

Esau, the hairy son, is your present objectified world . . the rough or sensibly felt; the present moment; the present environment; your present conception of yourself; in short, the world you know by reason of your objective senses.

Jacob, the smooth-skinned lad, the second son, is your desire or subjective state, an idea not yet embodied, a subjective state which is perceived and sensed but not objectively known or seen; a point in time and space removed from the present. In short, Jacob is your defined objective.

The smooth-skinned Jacob . . or subjective state seeking embodiment or the right of birth . . when properly felt or blessed by his father (when consciously felt and fixed as real), becomes objectified; and in so doing he supplants the rough, hairy Esau, or the former objectified state.

Two things cannot occupy a given place at one and the same time, and so as the invisible is made visible, the former visible state vanishes.

Your consciousness is the cause of your world. The conscious state in which you abide determines the kind of world in which you live.

Your present concept of yourself is now objectified as your environment, and this state is symbolized as Esau, the hairy, or sensibly felt; the first son.

That which you would like to be or possess is symbolized as your second son, Jacob, the smooth-skinned lad who is not yet seen but is subjectively senses and felt, and will, if properly touched, supplant his brother Esau, or your present world.

Always bear in mind the fact that Isaac, the father of these two sons, or states, is blind. He does not see his smooth-skinned son Jacob; he only feels him. And through the sense of feeling he actually believes Jacob, the subjective, to be Esau, the real, the objectified.

You do not see your desire objectively; you simply sense it (feel it) subjectively. You do not grope in space after a desirable state.

Like Isaac, you sit still and send your first son hunting by removing your attention from your objective world. Then in the absence of your first son, Esau, you invite the desirable state, your second son, Jacob, to come close so that you may feel it.

"Come close, my son, that I may feel you."

First, you are aware of it in your immediate environment; then you draw it closer and closer and closer until you sense it and feel it in your immediate presence so that it is real and natural to you.

"If two of you shall agree on earth as touching on any point that they shall ask, it shall be done for them of My Father, Which is in heaven."

The two agree, through the sense of feel, and the agreement is established on earth . . is objectified, is made real.

The two agreeing are Isaac and Jacob . . you and that which you desire; and the agreement is made solely on the sense of feeling.

Esau symbolizes your present objectified world whether it be pleasant or otherwise.

Jacob symbolizes any and every desire of your heart.

Isaac symbolizes your true self . . with your eyes closed to the present world . . in the act of sensing and feeling yourself to be or to possess that which you desire to be or to possess. The secret of Isaac, the sensing, feeling state, is simply the act of mentally separating the sensibly felt (your present physical state) from the insensibly felt (that which you would like to be).

With the objective senses tightly shut, Isaac made, and you can make, the insensibly felt, (the subjective state), seem real or sensibly known, for faith is knowledge.

Knowing the law of self-expression, the law by which the invisible is made visible, is not enough. *It must be applied*; and this is the method of application.

First: Send your first son Esau . . your present objectified world or problem . . hunting. This is accomplished simply by closing your eyes and taking your attention away from the objectified limitations. As your senses are removed from your objective world, it vanishes from your consciousness or goes hunting.

Second: With your eyes still closed and your attention removed from the world round about you, consciously fix the natural time and place for the realization of your desire.

With your objective senses closed to your present environment, you can sense and feel the reality of any point in time or space, for both are psychological and can be created at will.

It is vitally important that the natural time-space condition of Jacob, that is, the natural time and place for the realization of your desire, be first fixed in your consciousness.

If Sunday is the day on which the thing desired is to be realized, then Sunday must be fixed in consciousness now. Simply begin to feel that it is Sunday until the quietness and naturalness of Sunday is consciously established. You have definite associations with the days, weeks, months and seasons of the year. You have said time and again "Today feels like Sunday, or Monday, or Saturday; or this feels like Spring, or summer, or Fall, or Winter."

This should convince you that you have definite, conscious impressions that you associate with the days, weeks, and seasons of the year. Then because of these associations you can select any desirable time, and by recalling the conscious impression associated with such time, you can make a subjective reality of that time, now.

Do the same with space. If the room in which you are seated is not the room in which the thing desired would be naturally placed or realized, feel yourself seated in the room or place where it would be natural. Consciously fix this time space impression before you start the act of sensing and feeling the nearness, the reality, and the possession of the thing desired. It matters not whether the place desired be ten thousand miles away or only next door, you must fix in consciousness the fact that right where you are seated, is the desired place.

You do not make a mental journey; you collapse space. Sit quietly where you are, and make "thereness" . . "hereness." Close your eyes and feel that the very place where you are, is the place desired; feel and sense the reality of it until you are consciously impressed with this fact, for your knowledge of this fact is based solely on your subjective sensing.

Third: In the absence of Esau (the problem) and with the natural time-space established, you invite Jacob (the solution), to come and fill this space . . to come and supplant his brother.

In your imagination, see the thing desired. If you cannot visualize it, sense the general outline of it; contemplate it. Then mentally draw it close to you.

"Come close, my son, that I may feel you."

Feel the nearness of it; feel it to be in your immediate presence; feel the reality and solidity of it; feel it and see it naturally placed in the room in which you are seated; feel the thrill of actual accomplishment, and the joy of possession.

Now open your eyes.

This brings you back to the objective world . . the rough or sensibly felt world.

Your hairy son Esau has returned from the hunt and by his very presence tells you that you have been betrayed by your smooth-skinned son Jacob . . the subjective, psychologically felt. But, like Isaac, whose confidence was based upon the knowledge of this changeless law, you too will say,

*"I have made him thy Lord and all his brethren
have I given to him for servants".*

That is, even though your problems appears fixed and real, you have felt the subjective, psychological state to be real to the point of receiving the thrill of that reality; you have experienced the secret of creation, for you have felt the reality of the subjective.

You have fixed a definite psychological state which in spite of all opposition or precedent will objectify itself, thereby fulfilling the name of Jacob . . the supplanter.

Here are a few practical examples of this drama.

First: The blessing or making a thing real.

Sit in your living room and name a piece of furniture, rug or lamp that you would like to have in this particular room.

Look at that area of the room where you would place it if you had it. Close your eyes and let all that now occupies that area of the room vanish.

In your imagination see this area as empty space .. there is absolutely nothing there. Now begin to fill this space with the desired piece of furniture; sense and feel that you have it in this very area, imagine you are seeing that which you desired to see. Continue in this consciousness until you feel the thrill of possession.

Second. The blessing or the making of a place real.

You are now seated in your apartment in New York City, contemplating the joy that would be yours if you were on an ocean liner sailing across the great Atlantic.

"I go to prepare a place for you. And if I go and prepare a place for you, I will come again, and receive you unto myself; that where I am there ye may be also."

Your eyes are closed; you have consciously released the New York apartment and in its place you sense and feel that you are on an ocean liner. You are seated in a deck chair; there is nothing round you but the vast Atlantic.

Fix the reality of this ship and ocean so that in this state you can mentally recall the day when you were seated in your New York apartment dreaming of this day at sea. Recall the mental picture of yourself seated there in New York dreaming of this day. In your imagination see the memory picture of yourself back there in your New York apartment.

If you succeed in looking back on your New York apartment without consciously returning there, then you have successfully prepared the reality of this voyage.

Remain in this conscious state feeling the reality of the ship and the ocean; feel the joy of this accomplishment .. then open your eyes. You have gone and prepared the place; you have fixed a definite psychological state and where you are in consciousness there you shall be in body also.

Third: The blessing or making real of a point in time.

You consciously let go of this day, month or year, as the case may be, and you imagine that it is now that day, month or year which you desire to experience. You sense and feel the reality of the desired time by impressing upon yourself the fact that it is now accomplished.

As you sense the naturalness of this time, you begin to feel the thrill of having fully realized that which before you started this psychological journey in time you desired to experience at this time.

With the knowledge of your power to bless, you can open the doors of any prison . . the prison of illness or poverty or of a humdrum existence.

"The Spirit of the Lord God is upon me; because the Lord hath anointed me to preach good tidings unto the meek; he hath sent me to bind up the broken hearted, to proclaim liberty to the captives, and the opening of the prison to them that are bound."

Chapter 7

Chapter 7 of Freedom for All

Desire, The Word of God

"SO shall My word be that goeth forth out of My mouth; it shall not return unto Me void, but it shall accomplish that which I please, and it shall prosper in the thing whereunto I sent it."

God speaks to you through the medium of your basic desires. Your basic desires are words of promise or prophecies that contain within themselves the plan and power of expression.

By basic desire is meant your real objective. Secondary desires deal with the manner of realization. God, your I AM, speaks to you, the conditioned conscious state, through your basic desires. Secondary desires or ways of expression are the secrets of your I AM, the all wise Father. Your Father, I AM, reveals the first and last,

"I AM the beginning and the end"

but never does He reveal the middle or secret of His ways; that is, the first is revealed as the word, your basic desire.

The last is its fulfillment . . the word made flesh. The second or middle (the plan of unfoldment) is never revealed to man but remains forever the Father's secret.

"For I testify unto every man that heareth the words of the prophecy of this book, if any man shall add unto those things, God shall add unto him the plagues that are written in this book; and if any man shall take away from the words of the book of this prophecy, God shall take away his part out of the book of life."

The words of prophecy spoken of in the book of Revelation are your basic desires which must not be further conditioned. Man is constantly adding to and taking from these words. Not knowing that the basic desire contains the plan and power of expression man is always compromising and complicating his desire. Here is an illustration of what man does to the word of prophecy . . his desires.

Man desires freedom from his limitation or problem. The first thing he does after he defines his objective is to condition it upon something else. He begins to speculate on the manner of acquiring it.

Not knowing that the thing desired has a way of expression all of its own he starts planning how he is going to get it, thereby adding to the word of God.

If, on the other hand, he has no plan or conception as to the fulfillment of his desire, then he compromises his desire by modifying it. He feels that if he will be satisfied with less than his basic desire, then he might have a better chance of realizing it. In doing so he takes from the word of God.

Individuals and nations alike are constantly violating this law of their basic desire by plotting and planning the realization of their ambitions; they thereby add to the word of prophecy, or they compromise with their ideals, thus taking from the word of God. The inevitable result is death and plagues or failure and frustration as promised for such violations.

God speaks to man only through the medium of his basic desires. Your desires are determined by your conception of yourself. Of themselves they are neither good or evil.

"I know and am persuaded by the Lord Christ Jesus that there is nothing unclean of itself but to him that seeth anything to be unclean to him it is unclean."

Your desires are the natural and automatic result of your present conception of yourself. God, you unconditioned consciousness, is impersonal and no respecter of persons. Your unconditioned consciousness, God, gives to your conditioned consciousness, man, through the medium of your basic desires that which your conditioned state (your present conception of yourself) believes it needs.

As long as you remain in your present conscious state so long will you continue desiring that which you now desire. Change your conception of yourself and you will automatically change the nature of your desires.

Desires are states of consciousness seeking embodiment. They are formed by man's consciousness and can easily be expressed by the man who has conceived them. Desires are expressed when the man who has conceived them assumes the attitude of mind that would be his if the states desired were already expressed.

Now because desires regardless of their nature can be so easily expressed by fixed attitudes of mind, a word of warning must be given to those who have not yet realized the oneness of life, and who do not know the fundamental truth that consciousness is God, the one and only reality.

This warning was given to man in the famous Golden Rule . .

"Do unto others that which you would have them do unto you."

You may desire something for yourself or you may desire for another. If your desire concerns another make sure that the thing desired is acceptable to that other. The reason for this warning is that your consciousness is God, the giver of all gifts. Therefore, that which you feel and believe to be true of another is a gift you have given him.

The gift that is not accepted returns to the giver.

Be very sure then that you would love to possess the gift yourself, for if you fix a belief within yourself, as true of another, and he does not accept this state as true of himself, this unaccepted gift will embody itself within your world.

Always hear and accept as true of others that which you would desire for yourself. In so doing you are building heaven on earth.

"Do unto others as you would have them do unto you"

is based upon this law.

Only accept such states as true of others that you would willingly accept as true of yourself that you may constantly create heaven on earth.

Your heaven is defined by the state of consciousness in which you live, which state is made up of all that you accept as true of yourself and true of others. Your immediate environment is defined by your own conception of yourself plus your convictions regarding others which have not been accepted by them.

Your conception of another which is not his conception of himself is a gift returned to you.

Suggestions, like propaganda, are boomerangs unless they are accepted by those to whom they are sent.

So your world is a gift you have given to yourself.

The nature of the gift is determined by your conception of yourself plus the unaccepted gifts you offered others. Make no mistake about this; law is no respecter of persons.

Discover the law of self-expression and live by it; then you will be free.

With this understanding of the law, define your desire; know exactly what you want; make certain that it is desirable and acceptable.

The wise and disciplined man sees no barrier to the realization of his desire; he sees nothing to destroy. With a fixed attitude of mind he recognizes that the thing desired is already fully expressed, for he knows that a fixed subjective state, has ways and means of expressing itself, of which no man knows.

"Before they ask I have answered."

"I have ways ye know not of."

"My ways are past finding out."

The undisciplined man, on the other hand, constantly sees opposition to the fulfillment of his desire, and, because of the frustration, he forms desires of destruction which he firmly believes must be expressed before his basic desire can be realized.

When man discovers this law of one consciousness he will understand the great wisdom of the Golden Rule and so he will live by it and prove to himself that the kingdom of heaven is on earth.

You will realize why you should "do unto others that which you would have them do unto you." You will know why you should live by this Golden Rule because you will discover that it is just good common sense to do so since the rule is based upon life's changeless law and is no respecter of persons.

Consciousness is the one and only reality.

The world and all within it are states of consciousness objectified. Your world is defined by your conception of yourself, plus your conceptions of others, which are not their conceptions of themselves.

The story of the Passover is to help you turn your back on the limitations of the present and pass over into a better and freer state. The suggestion to

"Follow the man with the pitcher of water"

was given to the disciples to guide them to the last supper or the feast of the Passover. The man with the pitcher of water is the eleventh disciple, Simon of Canaan, the disciplined quality of mind which hears only dignified, noble and kindly states.

The mind that is disciplined to hear only the good, feasts upon good states, and so embodies the good on earth. If you, too, would attend the last supper . . the great feast of the Passover . . then follow this man.

Assume this attitude of mind symbolized as the

"man with the pitcher of water"

and you will live in a world that is really heaven on earth. The feast of the Passover is the secret of changing your consciousness. You turn your attention from your present conception of yourself and assume the consciousness of being that which you want to be, thereby passing from one state to another.

This feat is accomplished with the help of the twelve disciples, which are the twelve disciplined qualities of mind*

*"Your Faith is Your Fortune".

Chapter 8

Chapter 1 of Prayer: The Art of Believing

Law of Reversibility

> "Pray for my soul, more things are wrought
> by prayer than this world dreams of"
> (Tennyson)

Prayer is an art and requires practice. The first requirement is a controlled imagination. Parade and vain repetitions are foreign to prayer. Its exercise requires tranquility and peace of mind,

> "Use not vain repetitions,"

for prayer is done in secret

and

> *"thy Father which seeth in secret
> shall reward thee openly."*

The ceremonies that are customarily used in prayer are mere superstitions and have been invented to give prayer an air of solemnity. Those who do practice the art of prayer are often ignorant of the laws that control it. They attribute the results obtained to the ceremonies and mistake the letter for the spirit.

The essence of prayer is faith; but faith must be permeated with understanding to be given that active quality which it does not possess when standing alone.

> *"Therefore, get wisdom; and with all
> thy getting get understanding."*

This book is an attempt to reduce the unknown to the known, by pointing out conditions on which prayers are answered, and without which they cannot be answered. It defines the conditions governing prayer in laws that are simply a generalization of our observations

The universal law of reversibility is the foundation on which its claims are based.

Mechanical motion caused by speech was known for a long time before anyone dreamed of the possibility of an inverse transformation, that is, the reproduction of speech by mechanical motion (the phonograph). For a long time electricity was produced by friction without ever a thought that friction, in turn, could be produced by electricity.

Whether or not man succeeds in reversing the transformation of a force, he knows, nevertheless, that all transformations of force are reversible. If heat can produce mechanical motion, so mechanical motion can produce heat. If electricity produces magnetism, magnetism too can develop electric currents. If the voice can cause undulatory currents, so can such currents reproduce the voice, and so on. Cause and effect, energy and matter, action and reaction are the same and inter-convertible.

This law is of the highest importance, because it enables you to foresee the inverse transformation once the direct transformation is verified. If you knew how you would feel were you to realize your objective, then, inversely, you would know what state you could realize were you to awaken in yourself such feeling. The injunction, to pray believing that you already possess what you pray for, is based upon a knowledge of the law of inverse transformation.

If your realized prayer produces in you a definite feeling or state of consciousness, then, inversely, that particular feeling or state of consciousness must produce your realized prayer. Because all transformations of force are reversible, you should always assume the feeling of your fulfilled wish.

You should awaken within you the feeling that you are and have that which heretofore you desired to be and possess. This is easily done by contemplating the joy that would be yours were your objective an accomplished fact, so that you live and move and have your being in the feeling that your wish is realized.

The feeling of the wish fulfilled, if assumed and sustained, must objectify the state that would have created it.

This law explains why

*"Faith is the substance of things hoped for,
the evidence of things not seen"*

and why

*"He calleth things that are not seen as
though they were and things
that were not seen
become seen."*

Assume the feeling of your wish fulfilled and continue feeling that it is fulfilled until that which you feel objectifies itself.

If a physical fact can produce a psychological state, a psychological state can produce a physical fact. If the effect (a) can be produced by the cause (b), then inversely, the effect (b) can be produced by the cause (a).

Therefore I say unto you,

*"What things soever ye desire, when ye pray,
believe that ye have received them,
and ye shall have them"*

Chapter 9

Chapter 3 of Prayer: The Art of Believing

Imagination and Faith

Prayers are not successfully made unless there is a rapport between the conscious and subconscious mind of the operator. This is done through imagination and faith.

By the power of imagination all men, certainly imaginative men, are forever casting forth enchantments, and all men, especially unimaginative men, are continually passing under their power.

Can we ever be certain that it was not our mother while darning our socks who began that subtle change in our minds? If I can unintentionally cast an enchantment over persons, there is no reason to doubt that I am able to cast intentionally a far stronger enchantment.

Everything, that can be seen, touched, explained, argued over, is to the imaginative man nothing more than a means, for he functions, by reason of his controlled imagination, in the deep of himself where every idea exists in itself and not in relation to something else. In him there is no need for the restraints of reason. For the only restraint he can obey is the mysterious instinct that teaches him to eliminate all moods other than the mood of the fulfilled desire.

Imagination and faith are the only faculties of the mind needed to create objective conditions.

The faith required for the successful operation of the law of consciousness is a purely subjective faith and is attainable upon the cessation of active opposition on the part of the objective mind of the operator.

It depends on your ability to feel and accept as true what your objective senses deny.

Neither the passivity of the subject nor his conscious agreement with your suggestion is necessary, for without his consent or knowledge he can be given a subjective order which he must objectively express. It is a fundamental law of consciousness that by telepathy we can have immediate communion with another.

To establish rapport you call the subject mentally. Focus your attention on him and mentally shout his name just as you would to attract the attention of anyone. Imagine that he answered, and mentally hear his voice. Represent him to yourself inwardly in the state you want him to obtain. Then imagine that he is telling you in the tones of ordinary conversation what you want to hear. Mentally answer him. Tell him of your joy in witnessing his good fortune.

Having mentally heard with all the distinctness of reality that which you wanted to hear and having thrilled to the news heard, return to objective consciousness. Your subjective conversation must awaken what it affirmed.

"Thou shalt decree a thing and it shall be established unto thee."

It is not a strong will that sends the subjective word on its mission, so much as it is clear thinking and feeling, the truth of the state affirmed. When belief and will are in conflict, belief invariably wins.

"Not by might, nor by power, but by my spirit, saith the Lord of hosts."

It is not what you want that you attract; you attract what you believe to be true.

Therefore, get into the spirit of these mental conversations and give them the same degree of reality that you would a telephone conversation.

"If thou canst believe, all things are possible to him that believeth. Therefore, I say unto you, what things soever you desire, when you pray, believe that

ye received them, and ye shall have them."

The acceptance of the end wills the means. And the wisest reflection could not devise more effective means than those which are willed by the acceptance of the end. Mentally talk to your friends as though your desires for them were already realized.

Imagination is the beginning of the growth of all forms, and faith is the substance out of which they are formed.

By imagination, that which exists in latency or is asleep within the deep of consciousness is awakened and is given form.

The cures attributed to the influence of certain medicines, relics and places are the effects of imagination and faith. The curative power is not in the spirit that is in them, it is in the spirit in which they are accepted.

"The letter killeth, but the spirit giveth life."

The subjective mind is completely controlled by suggestion, so, whether the object of your faith be true or false, you will get the same results.

There is nothing unsound in the theory of medicine or in the claims of priesthood for their relics and holy places. The subjective mind of the patient accepts the suggestion of health conditioned on such states, and as soon as these conditions are met proceeds to realize health.

"According to your faith be it done unto you for all things are possible to him that believeth."

Confident expectation of a state is the most potent means of bringing it about. The confident expectation of a cure does that which no medical treatment can accomplish.

Failure is always due to an antagonistic auto-suggestion by the patient, arising from objective doubt of the power of medicine or relic, or from doubt of the truth of the theory.

Many of us, either from too little emotion or too much intellect, both of which are stumbling blocks in the way or prayer, cannot believe that which our sense deny.

To force ourselves to believe, will end in greater doubt. To avoid such counter-suggestions the patient should be unaware, objectively, of the suggestions which are made to him.

The most effective method of healing or influencing the behavior of others consists in what is known as "the silent or absent treatment." When the subject is unaware, objectively, of the suggestion given him there is no possibility of him setting up an antagonistic belief. It is not necessary that the patient know, objectively, that anything is being done for him.

From what is known of the subjective and objective processes of reasoning, it is better that he should not know objectively of that which is being done for him. The more completely the objective mind is kept in ignorance of the suggestion, the better will the subjective mind perform its functions.

The subject subconsciously accepts the suggestion and thinks he originates it, proving the truth of Spinoza's dictum, that we know not the causes that determine our actions.

The subconscious mind is the universal conductor which the operator modifies with his thoughts and feelings. Visible states are either the vibratory effects of subconscious vibrations within you or they are vibratory causes of the corresponding vibrations within you. A disciplined man never permits them to be causes unless they awaken in him the desirable states of consciousness.

With knowledge of the law of reversibility, the disciplined man transforms his world by imagining and feeling only what is lovely and of good report. The beautiful idea he awakens within himself shall not fail to arouse its affinity in others.

He knows the savior of the world is not a man but the manifestation that would save.

The sick man's savior is health, the hungry man's is food, the thirsty man's savior is water. He walks in the company of the savior, by assuming the feeling of his wish fulfilled.

By the law of reversibility, that all transformations of force are reversible, the energy or feeling awakened transforms itself into the state imagined. He never waits four months for the harvest. If in four months the harvest will awaken in him a state of joy, then, inversely, the joy of harvest now will awaken the harvest now.

"Now is the acceptable time to give beauty for ashes, joy for mourning, praise for the spirit of heaviness; that they might be called trees of righteousness, the planting of the Lord that he might be glorified."

Chapter 10

Chapter 3 of Out of this World

Power of Imagination

*"Ye shall know the truth, and the
truth shall make you free."*

Men claim that a true judgment must conform to the external reality to which it relates.

This means that if I, while imprisoned, suggest to myself that I am free and succeed in believing that I am free, it is true that I believe in my freedom; but it does not follow that I am free, for I may be the victim of illusion.

But, because of my own experiences, I have come to believe in so many strange things that I see little reason to doubt the truth of things that are beyond my experience.

The ancient teachers warned us not to judge from appearances because, said they, the truth need not conform to the external reality to which it relates.

They claimed that we bore false witness if we imagined evil against another, that no matter how real our belief appears to be, how truly it conforms to the external reality to which it relates, if it does not make free, the one of whom we hold the belief, it is untrue and therefore a false judgment.

We are called upon to deny the evidence of our senses and to imagine as true of our neighbor that which makes him free.

"Ye shall know the truth, and the truth shall make you free."

To know the truth of our neighbor we must assume that he is already that which he desires to be. Any concept we hold of another that is short of his fulfilled desire, will not make him free and therefore cannot be the truth.

Instead of learning my craft in schools where attending courses and seminars is considered a substitute for self-acquired knowledge, my schooling was devoted almost exclusively to the power of imagination. I sat for hours imagining myself to be other than that which my reason and my senses dictated until the imagined states were vivid as reality . . so vivid that passersby became but a part of my imagination and acted as I would have them.

By the power of imagination my fantasy led theirs and dictated to them their behavior and the discourse they held together while I was identified with my imagined state.

Man's imagination is the man himself, and the world as imagination sees it is the real world, but it is our duty to imagine all that is lovely and of good report.

"The Lord seeth not as man seeth, for man looketh upon the outward appearance, but the Lord looketh upon the heart."

"As a man thinketh in his heart so is he."

In meditation, when the brain grows luminous, I find my imagination endowed with the magnetic power to attract to me whatsoever I desire.

Desire is the power imagination uses to fashion life about me as I fashion it within myself. I first desire to see a certain person or scene, and then I look as though I were seeing that which I want to see, and the imagined state becomes objectively real. I desire to hear, and then I listen as though I were hearing, and the imagined voice speaks that which I dictate as though it had initiated the message.

I could give you many examples to prove my arguments, to prove that these imagined states do become physical realities; but I know that my examples will awaken in all who have not met the like or who are not inclined towards my arguments, a most natural incredulity.

Nevertheless, experience has convinced me of the truth of the statement,

"He calleth those things which be-not as though they were".

For I have, in intense meditation, called things that were not seen as though they were, and the unseen not only became seen, but eventually became physical realities.

By this method, first desiring and then imagining that we are experiencing that which we desire to experience, we can mold the future in harmony with our desire.

But let us follow the advice of the prophet and think only the lovely and the good, for the imagination waits on us as indifferently and as swiftly when our nature is evil as when it is good. From us spring forth good and evil.

"I have set before thee this day life and good, and death and evil."

Desire and imagination are the enchanter's wand of fable and they draw to themselves their own affinities. They break forth best when the mind is in a state akin to sleep.

I have written with some care and detail the method I use to enter the dimensionally larger world, but I shall give one more formula for opening the door of the larger world.

"In a dream, in a vision of the night, when deep sleep calleth upon men, in slumberings upon the bed; Then he openeth the ears of men, and sealeth their instruction."

In dream we are usually the servant of our vision rather than its master, but the internal fantasy of dream can be turned into an external reality.

In dream, as in meditation, we slip from this world into a dimensionally larger world, and I know that the forms in dream are not flat two-dimensional images which modern psychologists believe them to be. They are substantial realities of the dimensionally larger world, and I can lay hold of them. I have discovered that, if I surprise myself dreaming, I can lay hold of any inanimate or stationary form of the dream (a chair, a table, a stairway, a tree) and command myself to awake.

At the command to awake, while firmly holding on to the object of the dream, I am pulled through myself with the distinct feeling of awakening from dream. I awaken in another sphere holding the object of my dream, to find that I am no longer the servant of my vision but its master, for I am fully conscious and in control of the movements of my attention. It is in this fully conscious state, when we are in control of the direction of thought, that we call things that are not seen as though they were. In this state we call things by wishing and assuming the feeling of our wish fulfilled.

Unlike the world of three dimensions where there is an interval between our assumption and its fulfillment, in the dimensionally larger world there is an immediate realization of our assumption. The external reality instantly mirrors our assumption.

Here there is no need to wait four months till harvest. We look again as though we saw, and lo and behold, the fields are already white to harvest.

In this dimensionally larger world

"Ye shall not need to fight: set yourselves, stand ye still, and see the salvation of the Lord with you."

And because that greater world is slowly passing through our three-dimensional world, we can by the power of imagination mold our world in harmony with our desire. Look as though you saw, listen as though you heard; stretch forth your imaginary hand as though you touched . . and your assumptions will harden into facts.

To those who believe that a true judgment must conform to the external reality to which it relates, this will be foolishness and a stumbling-block. But I preach and practice the fixing in consciousness of that which man desires to realize.

Experience convinces me that fixed attitudes of mind which do not conform to the external reality to which they relate and are therefore called imaginary

"things which are not"

will, nevertheless,

"bring to nought things that are."

I do not wish to write a book of wonders, but rather to turn man's mind back to the one and only reality, that the ancient teachers worshiped as God.

All that was said of God, was in reality said of man's consciousness, so we may say,

"That, according as it is written, He that glorify, let him glory in his own consciousness."

No man needs help to direct him in the application of this law of consciousness.

"I AM" is the self-definition of the absolute. The root out of which everything prows.

"I AM the vine."

What is your answer to the eternal question,

"Who am I?"

Your answer determines the part you play in the world's drama. Your answer, that is, your concept of self, need not conform to the external reality to which it relates. This great truth is revealed in the statement,

"Let the weak say, I am strong."

Look back over the good resolutions with which many past new years are encumbered. They lived a little while and then they died. Why? Because they were severed from their root.

Assume that you are that which you want to be. Experience in imagination what you would experience in the flesh were you already that which you want to be. Remain faithful to your assumption, so that you define yourself as that which you have assumed.

Things have no life if they are severed from their roots, and our consciousness, our "I AMness," is the root of all that springs in our world.

"If ye believe not that I am he, ye shall die in your sins".

That is, if I do not believe that I am already that which I desire to be, then I remain as I am and die in my present concept of self.

There is no power, outside of the consciousness of man, to resurrect and make alive that which man desires to experience.

That man who is accustomed to call up at will, whatever images he pleases, will be, by virtue of the power of his imagination, master of his fate.

"I AM the resurrection, and the life: he that believeth in me, though he were dead, yet shall he live."

"Ye shall know the truth, and the truth shall make you free.

Chapter 11

Chapter 4 of Out of this World

No One to Change But Self

"And for their sakes I sanctify myself, that they also might be sanctified through the truth."

The ideal we serve and strive to attain could never be evolved from us were it not potentially involved in our nature. It is now my purpose to retell and to emphasize an experience of mine printed by me two years ago.

I believe these quotations from "The SEARCH" will help us to understand the operation of the law of consciousness, and show us that we have no one to change but self.

Once in an idle interval at sea I meditated on "the perfect state," and wondered what I would be, were I of too pure eyes to behold iniquity, if to me all things were pure and were I without condemnation.

As I became lost in this fiery brooding, I found myself lifted above the dark environment of the senses. So intense was the feeling I felt myself a being of fire dwelling in a body of air. Voices as from a heavenly chorus, with the exaltation of those who had been conquerors in a conflict with death, were. singing, "He is risen, He is risen," and intuitively I knew they meant me.

Then I seemed to be walking in the night. I soon came upon a scene that might have been the ancient Pool of Bethesda for in this place lay a great multitude of impotent folk . . blind, halt, withered, waiting not for the moving of the water as of tradition, but waiting for me.

As I came near, without thought or effort on my part they were, one after the other, molded as by the Magician of the Beautiful. Eyes, hands, feet . . all missing members . . were drawn from some invisible reservoir and molded in harmony with that perfection which I felt springing within me. When all were made perfect, the chorus exulted, "It is finished." Then the scene dissolved and I awoke.

I know this vision was the result of my intense meditation upon the idea of perfection, for my meditations invariably bring about union with the state contemplated. I had been so completely absorbed within the idea that for a while I had become what I contemplated, and the high purpose with which I had for that moment identified myself drew the companionship of high things and fashioned the vision in harmony with my inner nature.

The ideal with which we are united works by association of ideas to awaken a thousand moods to create a drama in keeping with the central idea.

My mystical experiences have convinced me that there is no way to bring about the outer perfection we seek other than by the transformation of ourselves. As soon as we succeed in transforming ourselves, the world will melt magically before our eyes and reshape itself in harmony with that which our transformation affirms.

In the divine economy nothing is lost. We cannot lose anything save by descent from the sphere where the thing has its natural life. There is no transforming power in death and, whether we are here or there, we fashion the world that surrounds us by the intensity of our imagination and feeling, and we illuminate or darken our lives by the concepts we hold of ourselves.

Nothing is more important to us than our conception of ourselves, and especially is this true of our concept of the dimensionally greater One within us.

Those who help or hinder us, whether they know it or not, are the servants of that law which shapes outward circumstances in harmony with our inner nature. It is our conception of ourselves which frees or constrains us, though it may use material agencies to achieve its purpose.

Because life molds the outer world to reflect the inner arrangement of our minds, there is no way of bringing about the outer perfection we seek other than by the transformation of ourselves.

No help cometh from without; the hills to which we lift our eyes are those of an inner range. It is thus to our own consciousness that we must turn as to the only reality, the only foundation on which all phenomena can be explained. We can rely absolutely on the justice of this law to give us only that which is of the nature of ourselves.

To attempt to change the world before we change our concept of ourselves is to struggle against the nature of things. There can be no outer change until there is first an inner change. "As within, so without."

I am not advocating philosophical indifference when I suggest that we should imagine ourselves as already that which we want to be, living in a mental atmosphere of greatness, rather than using physical means and arguments to bring about the desired change.

Everything we do, unaccompanied by a change of consciousness, is but futile readjustment of surfaces. However we toil or struggle, we can receive no more than our assumptions affirm. To protest against anything which happens to us is to protest against the law of our being and our rulership over our own destiny.

The circumstances of my life are too closely related to my conception of myself not to have been formed by my own spirit from some dimensionally larger storehouse of my being. If there is pain to me in these happenings, I should look within myself for the cause, for I am moved here and there and made to live in a world in harmony with my concept of myself.

Intense meditation brings about a union with the state contemplated, and during this union we see visions, have experiences and behave in keeping with our change of consciousness. This shows us that a transformation of consciousness will result in a change of environment and behavior.

All wars prove that violent emotions are extremely potent in precipitating mental rearrangements. Every great conflict has been followed by an era of materialism and greed in which the ideals for which the conflict ostensibly was waged are submerged. This is inevitable because war evokes hate which impels a descent in consciousness from the plane of the ideal to the level where the conflict is waged.

If we would become as emotionally aroused over our ideals as we become over our dislikes, we would ascend to the plane of our ideal as easily as we now descend to the level of our hates.

Love and hate have a magical transforming power, and we grow through their exercise into the likeness of what we contemplate. By intensity of hatred we create in ourselves the character we imagine in our enemies.

Qualities die for want of attention, so the unlovely states might best be rubbed out by imagining,

"beauty for ashes and joy for mourning"

rather than by direct attacks on the state from which we would be free.

"Whatsoever things are lovely and of good report, think on these things,"

for we become that with which we are en rapport.

There is nothing to change but our concept of self. As soon as we succeed in transforming self, our world will dissolve and reshape itself in harmony with that which our change affirms.

Chapter 12

Chapter 1 of Feeling is the Secret

Law and its Operation

The world, and all within it, is man's conditioned consciousness objectified.

Consciousness is the cause as well as the substance of the entire world. So it is to consciousness that we must turn if we would discover the secret of creation.

Knowledge of the law of consciousness and the method of operating this law will enable you to accomplish all you desire in life. Armed with a working knowledge of this law, you can build and maintain an ideal world.

Consciousness is the one and only reality, not figuratively but actually.

This reality may for the sake of clarity be likened unto a stream which is divided into two parts, the conscious and the subconscious. In order to intelligently operate the law of consciousness, it is necessary to understand the relationship between the conscious and the subconscious. The conscious is personal and selective; the subconscious is impersonal and non-selective. The conscious is the realm of effect; the subconscious is the realm of cause.

These two aspects are the male and female divisions of consciousness. The conscious is male; the subconscious is female.

The conscious generates ideas and impresses these ideas on the subconscious; the subconscious receives ideas and gives form and expression to them.

By this law . . first conceiving an idea and then impressing the idea conceived on the subconscious . . all things evolve out of consciousness; and without this sequence, there is not anything made that is made. The conscious impresses the subconscious, while the subconscious expresses all that is impressed upon it.

The subconscious does not originate ideas, but accepts as true those which the conscious mind feels to be true and, in a way known only to itself, objectifies the accepted ideas.

Therefore, through his power to imagine and feel and his freedom to choose the idea he will entertain, man has control over creation.

Control of the subconscious is accomplished through control of your ideas and feelings.

The mechanism of creation is hidden in the very depth of the subconscious, the female aspect or womb of creation.

The subconscious transcends reason and is independent of induction. It contemplates a feeling as a fact existing within itself and on this assumption proceeds to give expression to it.

The creative process begins with an idea and its cycle runs its course as a feeling and ends in a volition to act.

Ideas are impressed on the subconscious through the medium of feeling. No idea can be impressed on the subconscious until it is felt, but once felt . . be it good, bad or indifferent . . it must be expressed.

Feeling is the one and only medium through which ideas are conveyed to the subconscious. Therefore, the man who does not control his feeling may easily impress the subconscious with undesirable states.

By control of feeling is not meant restraint or suppression of your feeling, but rather the disciplining of self to imagine and entertain only such feeling as contributes to your happiness.

Control of your feeling is all important to a full and happy life. Never entertain an undesirable feeling, nor think sympathetically about wrong in any shape or form. Do not dwell on the imperfection of yourself or others. To do so is to impress the subconscious with these limitations. What you do not want done unto you, do not feel that it is done unto you or another. This is the whole law of a full and happy life. Everything else is commentary.

Every feeling makes a subconscious impression and, unless it is counteracted by a more powerful feeling of an opposite nature, must be expressed. The dominant of two feelings is the one expressed. I AM healthy is a stronger feeling than I will be healthy. To feel I will be is to confess I am not; I AM is stronger than I am not.

What you feel you are always dominates what you feel you would like to be; therefore, to be realized, the wish must be felt as a state that is rather than a state that is not.

Sensation precedes manifestation and is the foundation upon which all manifestation rests. Be careful of your moods and feelings, for there is an unbroken connection between your feelings and your visible world.

Your body is an emotional filter and bears the unmistakable marks of your prevalent emotions. Emotional disturbances, especially suppressed emotions, are the causes of all disease. To feel intensely about a wrong without voicing or expressing that feeling is the beginning of disease . . disease . . in both body and environment.

Do not entertain the feeling of regret or failure for frustration or detachment from your objective results in disease.

Think feelingly only of the state you desire to realize. Feeling the reality of the state sought and living and acting on that conviction is the way of all seeming miracles. All changes of expression are brought about through a change of feeling. A change of feeling is a change of destiny. All creation occurs in the domain of the subconscious.

What you must acquire, then, is a reflective control of the operation of the subconscious, that is, control of your ideas and feelings.

Chance or accident is not responsible for the things that happen to you, nor is predestined fate the author of your fortune or misfortune.

Your subconscious impressions determine the conditions of your world. The subconscious is not selective; it is impersonal and no respecter of persons. The subconscious is not concerned with the truth or falsity of your feeling. It always accepts as true that which you feel to be true.

Feeling is the assent of the subconscious to the truth of that which is declared to be true. Because of this quality of the subconscious there is nothing impossible to man.

Whatever the mind of man can conceive and feel as true, the subconscious can and must objectify. Your feelings create the pattern from which your world is fashioned, and a change of feeling is a change of pattern.

The subconscious never fails to express that which has been impressed upon it. The moment it receives an impression, it begins to work out the ways of its expression. It accepts the feeling impressed upon it, your feeling, as a fact existing within itself and immediately sets about to produce in the outer or objective world the exact likeness of that feeling.

The subconscious never alters the accepted beliefs of man. It out pictures them to the last detail whether or not they are beneficial.

To impress the subconscious with the desirable state, you must assume the feeling that would be yours had you already realized your wish. In defining your objective, you must be concerned only with the objective itself.

The manner of expression or the difficulties involved are not to be considered by you. To think feelingly on any state impresses it on the subconscious. Therefore, if you dwell on difficulties, barriers or delay, the subconscious, by its very non-selective nature, accepts the feeling of difficulties and obstacles as your request and proceeds to produce them in your outer world.

The subconscious is the womb of creation. It receives the idea unto itself through the feelings of man. It never changes the idea received, but always gives it form. Hence the subconscious out pictures the idea in the image and likeness of the feeling received.

To feel a state as hopeless or impossible is to impress the subconscious with the idea of failure.

Although the subconscious faithfully serves man it must not be inferred that the relation is that of a servant to a master as was anciently conceived. The ancient prophets called it the slave and servant of man.

St. Paul personified it as a "woman" and said: "The woman should be subject to man in everything."

The subconscious does serve man and faithfully gives form to his feelings. However, the subconscious has a distinct distaste for compulsion and responds to persuasion rather than to command; consequently, it resembles the beloved wife more than the servant.

"The husband is head of the wife,"

may not be true of man and woman in their earthly relationship but it is true of the conscious and the subconscious, or the male and female aspects of consciousness.

The mystery to which Paul referred when he wrote,

"This is a great mystery...
He that loveth his wife loveth himself.....
And they two shall be one flesh,"

is simply the mystery of consciousness.

Consciousness is really one and undivided but for creation's sake it appears to be divided into two.

The conscious (objective) or male aspect truly is the head and dominates the subconscious (subjective) or female aspect. However, this leadership is not that of the tyrant, but of the lover. So, by assuming the feeling that would be yours were you already in possession of your objective, the subconscious is moved to build the exact likeness of your assumption.

Your desires are not subconsciously accepted until you assume the feeling of their reality, for only through feeling is an idea subconsciously accepted and only through this subconscious acceptance is it ever expressed.

It is easier to ascribe your feeling to events in the world than to admit that the conditions of the world reflect your feeling. However, it is eternally true that the outside mirrors the inside.

"As within so without."

*"A man can receive nothing unless
it is given him from heaven,"*
and

"The kingdom of heaven is within you."

Nothing comes from without; all things come from within . . from the subconscious.

It is impossible for you to see other than the contents of your consciousness. Your world in its every detail is your consciousness objectified. Objective states bear witness of subconscious impressions. A change of impression results in a change of expression.

The subconscious accepts as true that which you feel as true, and because creation is the result of subconscious impressions, you, by your feeling, determine creation. You are already that which you want to be, and your refusal to believe this is the only reason you do not see it.

To seek on the outside for that which you do not feel you are, is to seek in vain, for we never find that which we want; we find only that which we are.

In short, you express and have only that which you are conscious of being or possessing.

"To him that hath it is given."

Denying the evidence of the senses and appropriating the feeling of the wish fulfilled is the way to the realization of your desire.

Mastery of self-control of your thoughts and feelings is your highest achievement.

However, until perfect self-control is attained, so that, in spite of appearances, you feel all that you want to feel, use sleep and prayer to aid you in realizing your desired states.

These are the two gateways into the subconscious.

Chapter 13

Chapter 4 of Feeling is the Secret

Spirit – Feeling

"Not by might, nor by power, but by my spirit, saith the Lord of hosts."

Get into the spirit of the state desired by assuming the feeling that would be yours were you already the one you want to be. As you capture the feeling of the state sought, you are relieved of all effort to make it so, for it is already so.

There is a definite feeling associated with every idea in the mind of man.

Capture the feeling associated with your realized wish by assuming the feeling that would be yours were you already in possession of the thing you desire, and your wish will objectify itself.

Faith is feeling,

"According to your faith (feeling) be it unto you."

You never attract that which you want but always that which you are. As a man is, so does he see.

*"To him that hath it shall be given
and
to him that hath not it shall be taken away..."*

That which you feel yourself to be you are, and you are given that which you are. So assume the feeling that would be yours were you already in possession of your wish, and your wish must be realized.

"So God created man in his own image, in the image of God created he him."

> *"Let this mind be in you which was also in Christ Jesus, who being in the form of God, thought it not robbery to be equal with God."*

You are that which you believe yourself to be.

Instead of believing in God or in Jesus . . believe you are God or you are Jesus.

> *"He that believeth on me the works that I do shall he do also"*

should be

> *"He that believes as I believe the works that I do shall he do also."*

Jesus found it not strange to do the works of God because he believed himself to be God.

> *"I and my Father are one."*

It is natural to do the works of the one you believe yourself to be. So live in the feeling of being the one you want to be and that you shall be.

When a man believes in the value of the advice given him and applies it, he establishes within himself the reality of success.

Chapter 14

Chapter 1 of The Power of Awareness

I AM

All things, when they are admitted, are made manifest by the light: for everything that is made manifest is light.

The "Light" is consciousness. Consciousness is one, manifesting in legions of forms or levels of consciousness.

There is no one that is not all that is, for consciousness, though expressed in an infinite series of levels, is not divisional. There is no real separation or gap in consciousness.

I AM cannot be divided. I may conceive myself to be a rich man, a poor man, a beggar man or a thief, but the center of my being remains the same, regardless of the concept I hold of myself.

At the center of manifestation, there is only one I AM manifesting in legions of forms or concepts of itself and

"I AM that I AM".

I AM is the self-definition of the absolute, the foundation on which everything rests. I AM is the first cause-substance.

I AM is the self-definition of God.

"I AM hath sent me unto you."

"I AM that I AM."

'Be still and know that I AM God."

I AM is a feeling of permanent awareness. The very center of consciousness is the feeling of I AM. I may forget who I am, where I am, what I am, but I cannot forget that I AM. The awareness of being remains, regardless of the degree of forgetfulness of who, where and what I am.

> *"I AM is that which,*
> *amid unnumbered forms,*
> *is ever the same."*

This great discovery of cause reveals that, good or bad, man is actually the arbiter of his own fate, and that it is his concept of himself that determines the world in which he lives [and his concept of himself is his reactions to life].

In other words, if you are experiencing ill health, knowing the truth about cause, you cannot attribute the illness to anything other than to the particular arrangement of the basic cause-substance, an arrangement which [was produced by your reactions to life, and] is defined by your concept "I am unwell". This is why you are told

"Let the weak man say, 'I AM strong'",

for by his assumption, the cause-substance . . I AM . . is rearranged and must, therefore, manifest that which its rearrangement affirms. This principle governs every aspect of your life, be it social, financial, intellectual, or spiritual.

I AM is that reality to which, whatever happens, we must turn for an explanation of the phenomena of life. It is I AM's concept of itself that determines the form and scenery of its existence.

Everything depends upon its attitude towards itself; that which it will not affirm as true of itself cannot awaken in its world.

That is, your concept of yourself, such as

"I AM strong", "I AM secure", "I AM loved",

determines the world in which you live. In other words, when you say, "I am a man, I am a father, I am an

American", you are not defining different I AM's; you are defining different concepts or arrangements of the one cause-substance, the one I AM. Even in the phenomena of nature, if the tree were articulate, it would say, "I am a tree, an apple tree, a fruitful tree".

When you know that consciousness is the one and only reality, conceiving itself to be something good, bad or indifferent, and becoming that which it conceived itself to be, you are free from the tyranny of second causes, free from the belief that there are causes outside of your own mind that can affect your life.

In the state of consciousness of the individual is found the explanation of the phenomena of life. If man's concept of himself were different, everything in his world would be different.

His concept of himself being what it is, everything in his world must be as it is.

Thus it is abundantly clear that there is only one I AM and you are that I AM.

And while I AM is infinite, you, by your concept of yourself, are displaying only a limited aspect of the infinite I AM.

> Build thee more stately mansions,
> O, my soul,
> As the swift seasons roll!
> Leave thy low-vaulted past!
> Let each new temple, nobler
> than the last,
> Shut thee from heaven with a
> dome more vast
> Till thou at length art free,
> Leaving thine outgrown shell by
> life's unresting sea!

Chapter 15

Chapter 2 of The Power of Awareness

Consciousness

It is only by a change of consciousness, by actually changing your concept of yourself, that you can

"build more stately mansions",

the manifestations of higher and higher concepts. By manifesting is meant experiencing the results of these concepts in your world.

It is of vital importance to understand clearly just what consciousness is.

The reason lies in the fact that consciousness is the one and only reality, it is the first and only cause-substance of the phenomena of life.

Nothing has existence for man save through the consciousness he has of it. Therefore, it is to consciousness you must turn, for it is the only foundation on which the phenomena of life can be explained.

If we accept the idea of a first cause, it would follow that the evolution of that cause could never result in anything foreign to itself.

That is, if the first cause-substance is light, all its evolutions, fruits and manifestations would remain light.

The first cause-substance being consciousness, all its evolutions, fruits and phenomena must remain consciousness. All that could be observed would be a higher or lower form or variation of the same thing. In other words, if your consciousness is the only reality, it must also be the only substance.

Consequently, what appears to you as circumstances, conditions and even material objects is really only the product of your own consciousness.

Nature, then, as a thing or a complex of things external to your mind, must be rejected. You and your environment cannot be regarded as existing separately.

You and your world are one.

Therefore, you must turn from the objective appearance of things to the subjective center of things, your consciousness, if you truly desire to know the cause of the phenomena of life, and how to use this knowledge to realize your fondest dreams.

In the midst of the apparent contradictions, antagonisms and contrasts of your life, there is only one principle at work, only your consciousness operating.

Difference does not consist in variety of substance, but in variety of arrangement of the same cause-substance, your consciousness.

The world moves with motiveless necessity. By this is meant that it has no motive of its own, but is under the necessity of manifesting your concept, the arrangement of your mind, and your mind is always arranged in the image of all you believe and consent to as true.

The rich man, poor man, beggar man or thief are not different minds, but different arrangements of the same mind, in the same sense that a piece of steel, when magnetized, differs not in substance from its demagnetized state, but in the arrangement and order of its molecules.

A single electron revolving in a specified orbit constitutes the unit of magnetism. When a piece of steel or anything else is demagnetized, the revolving electrons have not stopped. Therefore, the magnetism has not gone out of existence. There is only a rearrangement of the particles, so that they produce no outside or perceptible effect.

When particles are arranged at random, mixed up in all directions, the substance is said to be demagnetized; but when particles are marshaled in ranks so that a number of them face in one direction, the substance is a magnet.

Magnetism is not generated; it is displayed.

Health, wealth, beauty and genius are not created; they are only manifested by the arrangement of your mind, that is, by your concept of yourself, and your concept of yourself is all that you accept and consent to as true. What you consent to can only be discovered by an uncritical observation of your reactions to life.

Your reactions reveal where you live psychologically; and where you live psychologically determines how you live here in the outer visible world.

The importance of this in your daily life should be immediately apparent. The basic nature of the primal cause is consciousness.

Therefore, the ultimate substance of all things is consciousness.

Chapter 16

Chapter 3 of The Power of Awareness

Power of Assumption

Man's chief delusion is his conviction that there are causes other than his own state of consciousness.

All that befalls a man, all that is done by him, all that comes from him, happens as a result of his state of consciousness. A man's consciousness is all that he thinks and desires and loves, all that he believes is true and consents to.

That is why a change of consciousness is necessary before you can change your outer world.

Rain falls as a result of a change in the temperature in the higher regions of the atmosphere, so, in like manner, a change of circumstance happens as a result of a change in your state of consciousness.

"Be ye transformed by the renewing of your mind."

To be transformed, the whole basis of your thoughts must change. But your thoughts cannot change unless you have new ideas, for you think from your ideas.

All transformation begins with an intense, burning desire to be transformed. The first step in the

"renewing of the mind"

is desire. You must want to be different, and intend to be, before you can begin to change yourself. Then you must make your future dream a present fact.

You do this by assuming the feeling of your wish fulfilled. By desiring to be other than what you are, you can create an ideal of the person you want to be and assume that you are already that person. If this assumption is persisted in until it becomes your dominant feeling, the attainment of your ideal is inevitable.

The ideal you hope to achieve is always ready for an incarnation, but unless you yourself offer it human parentage, it is incapable of birth.

Therefore, your attitude should be one in which having desired to express a higher state . . you alone accept the task of incarnating this new and greater value of yourself.

In giving birth to your ideal, you must bear in mind that the methods of mental and spiritual knowledge are entirely different.

This is a point that is truly understood by probably not more than one person in a million.

You know a thing mentally by looking at it from the outside, by comparing it with other things, by analyzing it and defining it, by thinking of it; whereas you can know a thing spiritually only by becoming it, only by thinking from it.

You must be the thing itself and not merely talk about it or look at it. You must be like the moth in search of his idol, the flame,

> "who spurred with true desire, plunging at
> once into the sacred fire, folded his wings
> within, till he became one color and one
> substance with the flame. He only knew
> the flame who in it burned, and only he could
> tell who ne'er to tell returned."

Just as the moth in his desire to know the flame was willing to destroy himself, so must you in becoming a new person be willing to die to your present self.

You must be conscious of being healthy if you are to know what health is.

You must be conscious of being secure if you are to know what security is.

Therefore, to incarnate a new and greater value of yourself, you must assume that you already are what you want to be and then live by faith in this assumption, which is not yet incarnate in the body of your life, in confidence that this new value or state of consciousness will become incarnated through your absolute fidelity to the assumption that you are that which you desire to be.

This is what wholeness means, what integrity means.

They mean submission of the whole self to the feeling of the wish fulfilled in certainty that that new state of consciousness is the renewing of mind which transforms. There is no order in Nature corresponding to this willing submission of the self to the ideal beyond the self.

Therefore, it is the height of folly to expect the incarnation of a new and greater concept of self to come about by natural evolutionary process.

That which requires a state of consciousness to produce its effect obviously cannot be effected without such a state of consciousness, and in your ability to assume the feeling of a greater life, to assume a new concept of yourself, you possess what the rest of Nature does not possess . . imagination . . the instrument by which you create your world.

Your imagination is the instrument, the means, whereby your redemption from slavery, sickness, and poverty is effected.

If you refuse to assume the responsibility of the incarnation of a new and higher concept of yourself, then you reject the means, the only means, whereby your redemption, that is, the attainment of your ideal, can be effected.

Imagination is the only redemptive power in the universe.

However, your nature is such that it is optional to you whether you remain in your present concept of yourself (a hungry being longing for freedom, health, and security) or choose to become the instrument of your own redemption, imagining yourself as that which you want to be, and thereby satisfying your hunger and redeeming yourself.

> "O, be strong then, and brave,
> pure, patient and true;
> The work that is yours let no
> other hand do.
> For the strength for all need is
> faithfully given
> From the fountain within you –
> The Kingdom of Heaven."

Chapter 17

Chapter 4 of The Power of Awareness

Desire

The changes which take place in your life as a result of your changed concept of yourself always appear to the unenlightened to be the result, not of a change of your consciousness, but of chance, outer cause, or coincidence.

However, the only fate governing your life is the fate determined by your own concepts, your own assumptions; for an assumption, though false, if persisted in, will harden into fact.

The ideal you seek and hope to attain will not manifest itself, will not be realized by you until you have imagined that you are already that ideal.

There is no escape for you except by a radical psychological transformation of yourself, except by your assumption of the feeling of your wish fulfilled. Therefore, make results or accomplishments the crucial test of your ability to use your imagination.

Everything depends on your attitude towards yourself. That which you will not affirm as true of yourself can never be realized by you, for that attitude alone is the necessary condition by which you realize your goal.

All transformation is based upon suggestion, and this can work only where you lay yourself completely open to an influence.

You must abandon yourself to your ideal as a woman abandons herself to love, for complete abandonment of self to it is the way to union with your ideal.

You must assume the feeling of the wish fulfilled until your assumption has all the sensory vividness of reality. You must imagine that you are already experiencing what you desire. That is, you must assume the feeling of the fulfillment of your desire until you are possessed by it and this feeling crowds all other ideas out of your consciousness.

The man who is not prepared for the conscious plunge into the assumption of the wish fulfilled in the faith that it is the only way to the realization of his dream is not yet ready to live consciously by the law of assumption, although there is no doubt that he does live by the law of assumption unconsciously.

But for you, who accept this principle and are ready to live by consciously assuming that your wish is already fulfilled, the adventure of life begins.

To reach a higher level of being, you must assume a higher concept of yourself. If you will not imagine yourself as other than what you are, then you remain as you are,

*"for if ye believe not that I AM He,
ye shall die in your sins."*

If you do not believe that you are He, the person you want to be, then you remain as you are.

Through the faithful systematic cultivation of the feeling of the wish fulfilled, desire becomes the promise of its own fulfillment.

The assumption of the feeling of the wish fulfilled makes the future dream a present fact.

Chapter 18

Chapter 5 of The Power of Awareness

The Truth That Sets You Free

The drama of life is a psychological one, in which all the conditions, circumstances and events of your life are brought to pass by your assumptions.

Since your life is determined by your assumptions, you are forced to recognize the fact that you are either a slave to your assumptions or their master. To become the master of your assumptions is the key to undreamed of freedom and happiness.

You can attain this mastery by deliberate conscious control of your imagination.

You determine your assumptions in this way:

Form a mental image, a picture of the state desired, of the person you want to be. Concentrate your attention upon the feeling that you are already that person. First, visualize the picture in your consciousness. Then feel yourself to be in that state as though it actually formed your surrounding world.

By your imagination that which was a mere mental image is changed into a seemingly solid reality.

The great secret is a controlled imagination and a well sustained attention firmly and repeatedly focused on the object to be accomplished. It cannot be emphasized too much that, by creating an ideal within your mental sphere, by assuming that you are already that ideal, you identify yourself with it and thereby transform yourself into its image, thinking from the ideal instead of thinking of the ideal.

Every state is already there as "mere possibilities" as long as we think of them, but as overpoweringly real when we think from them.

This was called by the ancient teachers
"Subjection to the will of God"

or

"Resting in the Lord",

and the only true test of "Resting in the Lord" is that all who do rest are inevitably transformed into the image of that in which they rest, thinking from the wish fulfilled.

You become according to your resigned will, and your resigned will is your concept of yourself and all that you consent to and accept as true. You, assuming the feeling of your wish fulfilled and continuing therein, take upon yourself the results of that state; not assuming the feeling of your wish fulfilled, you are ever free of the results.

When you understand the redemptive function of imagination, you hold in your hands the key to the solution of all your problems.

Every phase of your life is made by the exercise of your imagination. Determined imagination alone is the means of your progress, of the fulfilling of your dreams. It is the beginning and end of all creating.

The great secret is a controlled imagination and a well sustained attention firmly and repeatedly focused on the feeling of the wish fulfilled until it fills the mind and crowds all other ideas out of consciousness.

What greater gifts could be given you than to be told the Truth that will set you free?

The Truth that sets you free is that you can experience in imagination what you desire to experience in reality, and by maintaining this experience in imagination, your desire will become an actuality.

You are limited only by your uncontrolled imagination and lack of attention to the feeling of your wish fulfilled. When the imagination is not controlled and the attention not steadied on the feeling of the wish fulfilled, then no amount of prayer or piety or invocation will produce the desired effect.

When you can call up at will whatsoever image you please, when the forms of your imagination are as vivid to you as the forms of nature, you are master of your fate.

You must stop spending your thoughts, your time and your money. Everything in life must be an investment.*

> Visions of beauty and splendor,
> Forms of a long-lost race,
> Sounds and faces and voices,
> From the fourth dimension of space –
> And on through the universe boundless,
> Our thoughts go lightning shod –
> Some call it imagination,
> And others call it God.

* Neville follows this with the date April 12, 1953. In Awakened Imagination (1954), he would write,

"On the morning of April 12, 1953, my wife was awakened by the sound of a great voice of authority speaking within her and saying, 'You must stop spending your thoughts, time, and money. Everything in life must be an investment'. To spend is to waste, to squander, to layout without return. To invest is to lay out for a purpose from which a profit is expected. This revelation of my wife is about the importance of the moment. It is about the transformation of the moment... It is only what is done now that counts... Whenever we assume the feeling of being what we want to be, we are investing". (Chapter. 5 - Awakened Imagination)

Chapter 19

Chapter 10 of The Power of Awareness

Creation

"I AM God, declaring the end from the beginning, and from ancient times, things that are not yet done."

Creation is finished.

Creativeness is only a deeper receptiveness, for the entire contents of all time and all space, while experienced in a time sequence, actually coexist in an infinite and eternal now.

In other words, all that you ever have been or ever will be, in fact, all that mankind ever was or ever will be, exists now.

This is what is meant by creation, and the statement that creation is finished means nothing is ever to be created, it is only to be manifested.

What is called creativeness is only becoming aware of what already is. You simply become aware of increasing portions of that which already exists.

The fact that you can never be anything that you are not already or experience anything not already existing explains the experience of having an acute feeling of having heard before what is being said, or having met before the person being met for the first time, or having seen before a place or thing being seen for the first time.

The whole of creation exists in you, and it is your destiny to become increasingly aware of its infinite wonders and to experience ever greater and grander portions of it.

If creation is finished, and all events are taking place now, the question that springs naturally to the mind is "what determines your time track?"

That is, what determines the events which you encounter?

And the answer is your concept of yourself. Concepts determine the route that attention follows.

Here is a good test to prove this fact. Assume the feeling of your wish fulfilled and observe the route that your attention follows. You will observe that as long as you remain faithful to your assumption, so long will your attention be confronted with images clearly related to that assumption.

For example;

if you assume that you have a wonderful business, you will notice how in your imagination, your attention is focused on incident after incident relating to that assumption. Friends congratulate you, tell you how lucky you are. Others are envious and critical. From there, your attention goes to larger offices, bigger bank balances, and many other similarly related events.

Persistence in this assumption will result in actually experiencing in fact that which you assumed.

The same is true regarding any concept. If your concept of yourself is that you are a failure, you would encounter in your imagination a whole series of incidents in conformance to that concept.

Thus it is clearly seen how you, by your concept of yourself, determine your present, that is, the particular portion of creation which you now experience, and your future, that is, the particular portion of creation which you will experience.

Chapter 20

Chapter 17 of The Power of Awareness

All Things Are Possible

It is of great significance that the truth of the principles outlined in this book have been proven time and again by the personal experiences of the Author.

Throughout the past twenty-five years, he has applied these principles and proved them successful in innumerable instances. He attributes to an unwavering assumption of his wish already being fulfilled every success that he has achieved.

He was confident that, by these fixed assumptions, his desires were predestined to be fulfilled. Time and again, he assumed the feeling of his wish fulfilled and continued in his assumption until that which he desired was completely realized.

Live your life in a sublime spirit of confidence and determination; disregard appearances, conditions, in fact all evidence of your senses that deny the fulfillment of your desire.

Rest in the assumption that you are already what you want to be, for, in that determined assumption, you and your Infinite Being are merged in creative unity, and with your Infinite Being (God) all things are possible. God never fails.

"For who can stay His hand or say
unto Him, What doest thou?"

Through the mastery of your assumptions, you are in very truth enabled to master life.

It is thus that the ladder of life is ascended: thus the ideal is realized.

The clue to the real purpose of life is to surrender yourself to your ideal with such awareness of its reality that you begin to live the life of the ideal and no longer your own life as it was prior to this surrender.

"He calleth things that are not seen as though they were, and the unseen becomes seen".

Each assumption has its corresponding world.

If you are truly observant, you will notice the power of your assumptions to change circumstances which appear wholly immutable.

You, by your conscious assumptions, determine the nature of the world in which you live.

Ignore the present state and assume the wish fulfilled.

Claim it; it will respond.

The law of assumption is the means by which the fulfillment of your desires may be realized.

Every moment of your life, consciously or unconsciously, you are assuming a feeling. You can no more avoid assuming a feeling than you can avoid eating and drinking.

All you can do is control the nature of your assumptions. Thus it is clearly seen that the control of your assumption is the key you now hold to an ever expanding, happier, more noble life.

Chapter 21

Chapter 1 of Awakened Imagination & the Search

Who is Your Imagination?

> I rest not from my great task
> to open the Eternal Worlds, to open
> the immortal Eyes
> of Man inwards into the Worlds of
> thought: into Eternity
> ever expanding in the Bosom of
> God, the Human Imagination.
> . . . Blake

Certain words in the course of long use gather so many strange connotations that they almost cease to mean anything at all.

Such a word is imagination.

This word is made to serve all manner of ideas, some of them directly opposed to one another. Fancy, thought, hallucination, suspicion: indeed, so wide is its use and so varied its meanings, the word imagination has no status nor fixed significance.

For example, we ask a man to "use his imagination", meaning that his present outlook is too restricted and therefore not equal to the task. In the next breath, we tell him that his ideas are "pure imagination", thereby implying that his ideas are unsound.

We speak of a jealous or suspicious person as a "victim of his own imagination", meaning that his thoughts are untrue. A minute later we pay a man the highest tribute by describing him as a "man of imagination".

Thus the word imagination has no definite meaning. Even the dictionary gives us no help.

It defines imagination as:

(1) the picturing power or act of the mind, the constructive or creative principle;

(2) a phantasm;

(3) an irrational notion or belief;

(4) planning, plotting or scheming as involving mental construction.

I identify the central figure of the Gospels with human imagination, the power which makes the forgiveness of sins, the achievement of our goals, inevitable.

> "All things were made by Him; and without
> Him was not anything made that was made."

There is only one thing in the world, Imagination, and all our deformations of it.

> "He is despised and rejected of men; a man of
> sorrows, and acquainted with grief."

Imagination is the very gateway of reality.

"Man", said Blake,

"is either the ark of God or a phantom of the earth and of the water".

"Naturally he is only a natural organ subject to Sense".

"The Eternal Body of Man is The Imagination: that is God himself, The Divine Body. יש׳ [yod, shin, ayin; from right to the left]: Jesus: we are His Members".

I know of no greater and truer definition of the Imagination than that of Blake.

By imagination we have the power

to be anything we desire to be.

Through imagination, we disarm and transform the violence of the world. Our most intimate as well as our most casual relationships become imaginative, as we awaken to "the mystery hid from the ages", that Christ in us is our imagination.

We then realize that only as we live by imagination can we truly be said to live at all.

I want this book to be the simplest, clearest, frankest work I have the power to make it, that I may encourage you to function imaginatively, that you may open your "Immortal Eyes inwards into the Worlds of Thought", where you behold every desire of your heart as ripe grain "white already to harvest".

*"I am come that they might have life,
and that they might have it more abundantly."*

The abundant life that Christ promised us is ours to experience now, but not until we have the sense of Christ as our imagination can we experience it.

*"The mystery hid from the ages...
Christ in you, the hope of glory,"*

is your imagination.

This is the mystery which I am ever striving to realize more keenly myself and to urge upon others.

Imagination is our redeemer,

"the Lord from Heaven"
born of man but not begotten of man.

Every man is Mary and birth to Christ must give.

If the story of the Immaculate Conception and birth of Christ appears irrational to man, it is only because it is misread as biography, history, and cosmology, and the modern explorers of the imagination do not help by calling It the unconscious or subconscious mind.

Imagination's birth and growth is the gradual transition from a God of tradition to a God of experience. If the birth of Christ (imagination) in man seems slow, it is only because man is unwilling to let go the comfortable but false anchorage of tradition.

When imagination is discovered as the first principle of religion, the stone of literal understanding will have felt the rod of Moses and, like the rock of Zin, issue forth the water of psychological meaning to quench the thirst of humanity; and all who take the proffered cup and live a life according to this truth will transform the water of psychological meaning into the wine of forgiveness.

Then, like the good Samaritan, they will pour it on the wounds of all.

The Son of God is not to be found in history, nor in any external form. He can only be found as the imagination of him in whom His presence becomes manifest.

O, would thy heart but be a manger for His birth!
God would once more become a child on earth.

Man is the garden in which this only-begotten Son of God sleeps. He awakens this Son by lifting his imagination up to heaven and clothing men in godlike stature. We must go on imagining better than the best we know.

Man in the moment of his awakening to the imaginative life must meet the test of Sonship.

"Father, reveal Thy Son in me"

And

"It pleased God to reveal His Son in me".

The supreme test of Sonship is the forgiveness of sin. The test that your imagination is Christ Jesus, the Son of God, is your ability to forgive sin.

Sin means missing one's mark in life, falling short of one's ideal, failing to achieve one's aim.

Forgiveness means identification of man with his ideal or aim in life.

This is the work of awakened imagination, the supreme work, for it tests man's ability to enter into and partake of the nature of his opposite.

"Let the weak man say, I AM strong."

Reasonably, this is impossible. Only awakened imagination can enter into and partake of the nature of its opposite.

This conception of Christ Jesus as human imagination raises these fundamental questions: Is imagination a power sufficient, not merely to enable me to assume that I am strong, but is it also of itself capable of executing the idea?

Suppose that I desire to be in some other place or situation. Could I, by imagining myself into such a state and place, bring about their physical realization?

Suppose I could not afford the journey and suppose my present social and financial status oppose the idea that I want to realize. Would imagination be sufficient of itself to incarnate these desires? Does imagination comprehend reason? By reason, I mean deductions from the observations of the senses.

Does it recognize the external world of facts?

In the practical way of everyday life is imagination a complete guide to behavior?

Suppose I am capable of acting with continuous imagination, that is, suppose I am capable of sustaining the feeling of my wish fulfilled, will my assumption harden into fact?

And, if it does harden into fact, shall I on reflection find that my actions through the period of incubation have been reasonable? Is my imagination a power sufficient, not merely to assume the feeling of the wish fulfilled, but is it also of itself capable of incarnating the idea?

After assuming that I am already what I want to be, must I continually guide myself by reasonable ideas and actions in order to bring about the fulfillment of my assumption?

Experience has convinced me that an assumption, though false, if persisted in, will harden into fact, that continuous imagination is sufficient for all things, and all my reasonable plans and actions will never make up for my lack of continuous imagination.

Is it not true that the teachings of the Gospels can only be received in terms of faith and that the Son of God is constantly looking for signs of faith in people, that is, faith in their own imagination?

Is not the promise

"Believe that ye receive and ye shall receive."
the same as
"Imagine that you are and you shall be"?

Was it not an imaginary state in which Moses

"Endured, as seeing Him who is invisible"?

Was it not by the power of his own imagination that he endured?

Truth depends upon the intensity of the imagination, not upon external facts. Facts are the fruit bearing witness of the use or misuse of the imagination.

Man becomes what he imagines.

He has a self-determined history. Imagination is the way, the truth, the life revealed. We cannot get hold of truth with the logical mind. Where the natural man of sense sees a bud, imagination sees a rose full-blown.

Truth cannot be encompassed by facts. As we awaken to the imaginative life, we discover that to imagine a thing is to make it so, that a true judgment need not conform to the external reality to which it relates.

The imaginative man does not deny the reality of the sensuous outer world of Becoming, but he knows that it is the inner world of continuous Imagination that is the force by which the sensuous outer world of Becoming is brought to pass.

He sees the outer world and all its happenings as projections of the inner world of Imagination. To him, everything is a manifestation of the mental activity which goes on in man's imagination, without the sensuous reasonable man being aware of it.

But he realizes that every man must become conscious of this inner activity and see the relationship between the inner causal world of imagination and the sensuous outer world of effects.

It is a marvelous thing to find that you can imagine yourself into the state of your fulfilled desire and escape from the jails which ignorance built.

The Real Man is a Magnificent Imagination.

It is this self that must be awakened.

"Awake thou that sleepest, and arise from the dead, and Christ shall give thee light."

The moment man discovers that his imagination is Christ, he accomplishes acts which on this level can only be called miraculous.

But until man has the sense of Christ as his imagination,

> *"You did not choose me,*
> *I have chosen you."*

He will see everything in pure objectivity without any subjective relationship.

Not realizing that all that he encounters is part of himself, he rebels at the thought that he has chosen the conditions of his life, that they are related by affinity to his own mental activity.

Man must firmly come to believe that reality lies within him and not without.

Although others have bodies, a life of their own, their reality is rooted in you, ends in you, as yours ends in God.

Chapter 22

Chapter 3: of Awakened Imagination & the Search

Highways of the Inner World

> *"And the children struggled within her... and the Lord said unto her, two nations are in thy womb, and two manner of people shall be separated from thy bowels; and the one people shall be stronger than the other people; and the elder shall serve the younger."*

Duality is an inherent condition of life. Everything that exists is double. Man is a dual creature with contrary principles embedded in his nature.

They war within him and present attitudes to life which are antagonistic. This conflict is the eternal enterprise, the war in heaven, the never ending struggle of the younger or inner man of imagination to assert His supremacy over the elder or outer man of sense.

"The first shall be last and the last shall be first."

"He it is, Who coming after me is preferred before me."

"The second Man is the Lord from heaven."

Man begins to awake to the imaginative life the moment he feels the presence of another being in himself.

> *"In your limbs lie nations twain, rival races from their birth; one the mastery shall gain, the younger o'er the elder reign."*

There are two distinct centers of thought or outlooks on the world possessed by every man.

The Bible speaks of these two outlooks as natural and spiritual.

Highways of the Inner World

> *"The natural man receiveth not the things*
> *of the Spirit of God: for they are foolishness*
> *unto him: neither can he know them, because*
> *they are spiritually discerned."*

Man's inner body is as real in the world of subjective experience as his outer physical body is real in the world of external realities, but the inner body expresses a more fundamental part of reality. This existing inner body of man must be consciously exercised and directed. The inner world of thought and feeling to which the inner body is attuned has its real structure and exists in its own higher space.

There are two kinds of movement, one that is according to the inner body and another that is according to the outer body. The movement which is according to the inner body is causal, but the outer movement is under compulsion.

The inner movement determines the outer which is joined to it, bringing into the outer a movement that is similar to the actions of the inner body. Inner movement is the force by which all events are brought to pass. Outer movement is subject to the compulsion applied to it by the movement of the inner body.

Whenever the actions of the inner body match the actions which the outer must take to appease desire, that desire will be realized.

Construct mentally a drama which implies that your desire is realized and make it one which involves movement of self. Immobilize your outer physical self. Act precisely as though you were going to take a nap, and start the predetermined action in imagination.

A vivid representation of the action is the beginning of that action. Then, as you are falling asleep, consciously imagine yourself into the scene. The length of the sleep is not important, a short nap is sufficient, but carrying the action into sleep thickens fancy into fact.

At first your thoughts may be like rambling sheep that have no shepherd. Don't despair. Should your attention stray seventy times seven, bring it back seventy times seven to its predetermined course until from sheer exhaustion it follows the appointed path.

The inner journey must never be without direction. When you take to the inner road, it is to do what you did mentally before you started. You go for the prize you have already seen and accepted.

In The Road to Xanadu, Professor John Livingston Lowes says:

"But I have long had the feeling, which this study had matured to a conviction, that Fancy and Imagination are not two powers at all, but one.

The valid distinction which exists between them lies, not in the materials with which they operate, but in the degree of intensity of the operant power itself. Working at high tension, the imaginative energy assimilates and transmutes; keyed low, the same energy aggregates and yokes together those images which at its highest pitch, it merges indissolubly into one."

Fancy assembles, imagination fuses.

Here is a practical application of this theory.

A year ago, a blind girl living in the city of San Francisco found herself confronted with a transportation problem. A rerouting of buses forced her to make three transfers between her home and her office. This lengthened her trip from fifteen minutes to two hours and fifteen minutes. She thought seriously about this problem and came to the decision that a car was the solution. She knew that she could not drive a car but felt that she could be driven in one.

Putting this theory to the test that "whenever the actions of the inner self correspond to the actions which the outer, physical self must take to appease desire, that desire will be

The Very Best of Neville - Chapter 22 - Highways of the Inner World

realized", she said to herself, "I will sit here and imagine that I am being driven to my office."

Sitting in her living room, she began to imagine herself seated in a car. She felt the rhythm of the motor. She imagined that she smelled the odor of gasoline, felt the motion of the car, touched the sleeve of the driver and felt that the driver was a man. She felt the car stop, and turning to her companion, said, "Thank you very much, sir."

To which he replied, "The pleasure is all mine."

Then she stepped from the car and heard the door snap shut as she closed it.

She told me that she centered her imagination on being in a car and, although blind, viewed the city from her imaginary ride. She did not think of the ride. She thought from the ride and all that it implied.

This controlled and subjectively directed purposive ride raised her imagination to its full potency. She kept her purpose ever before her, knowing there was cohesion in purposive inner movement. In these mental journeys, an emotional continuity must be sustained, the emotion of fulfilled desire. Expectancy and desire were so intensely joined that they passed at once from a mental state into a physical act.

The inner self moves along the predetermined course best when the emotions collaborate. The inner self must be fired, and it is best fired by the thought of great deeds and personal gain. We must take pleasure in our actions.

On two successive days, the blind girl took her imaginary ride, giving it all the joy and sensory vividness of reality. A few hours after her second imaginary ride, a friend told her of a story in the evening paper. It was a story of a man who was interested in the blind. The blind girl phoned him and stated her problem. The very next day, on his way home, he stopped in at a bar and while there had the urge to tell the story of the blind girl to his friend the proprietor. A total stranger, on hearing the story, volunteered to drive the blind girl home every day. The man who told the story then said, "If you will take her home, I will take her to work."

This was over a year ago, and since that day, this blind girl has been driven to and from her office by these two gentlemen.

Now, instead of spending two hours and fifteen minutes on three buses, she is at her office in less than fifteen minutes. And on that first ride to her office, she turned to her good Samaritan and said, "Thank you very much, sir"; and he replied, "The pleasure is all mine."

Thus, the objects of her imagination were to her the realities of which the physical manifestation was only the witness. The determinative animating principle was the imaginative ride. Her triumph could be a surprise only to those who did not know of her inner ride. She mentally viewed the world from this imaginative ride with such a clearness of vision that every aspect of the city attained identity.

These inner movements not only produce corresponding outer movements: this is the law which operates beneath all physical appearances. He who practices these exercises of bilocation will develop unusual powers of concentration and quiescence and will inevitably achieve waking consciousness on the inner and dimensionally larger world.

Actualizing strongly, she fulfilled her desire, for, viewing the city from the feeling of her wish fulfilled, she matched the state desired and granted that to herself which sleeping men ask of God.

To realize your desire, an action must start in your imagination, apart from the evidence of the senses, involving movement of self and implying fulfillment of your desire. Whenever it is the action which the outer self takes to appease desire, that desire will be realized.

The movement of every visible object is caused not by things outside the body, but by things within it, which operate from within outward. The journey is in yourself. You travel along the highways of the inner world. Without inner movement, it is impossible to bring forth anything. Inner action is introverted sensation.

If you will construct mentally a drama which implies that you have realized your objective, then close your eyes and drop your thoughts inward, centering your imagination all the while in the predetermined action and partake in that action, you will become a self-determined being.

Inner action orders all things according to the nature of itself. Try it and see whether a desirable ideal once formulated is possible, for only by this process of experiment can you realize your potentialities.

It is thus that this creative principle is being realized. So the clue to purposive living is to center your imagination in the action and feeling of fulfilled desire with such awareness, such sensitiveness, that you initiate and experience movement upon the inner world.

Ideas only act if they are felt, if they awaken inner movement. Inner movement is conditioned by self-motivation, outer movement by compulsion.

"Wherever the sole of your foot shall tread, the same give I unto you."

and remember,

"The Lord thy God in the midst of thee is mighty."

Chapter 23

Chapter 4 of Awakened Imagination & the Search

The Pruning Shears of Revision

"The second Man is the Lord from Heaven."

Never will he say caterpillars. He'll say, "There's a lot of butterflies-as-is-to-be on our cabbages, Prue." He won't say, "It's winter." He'll say, "Summer's sleeping." And there's no bud little enough nor sad-colored enough for Kester not to callen it the beginnings of the blow.
. . . Mary Webb, Precious Bane

The very first act of correction or cure is always "revise". One must start with oneself. It is one's attitude that must be changed.

What we are, that only can we see.
. . . Emerson

It is a most healthy and productive exercise to daily relive the day as you wish you had lived it, revising the scenes to make them conform to your ideals.

For instance,

suppose today's mail brought disappointing news. Revise the letter. Mentally rewrite it and make it conform to the news you wish you had received. Then, in imagination, read the revised letter over and over again.

This is the essence of revision, and revision results in repeal.

The one requisite is to arouse your attention in a way and to such intensity that you become wholly absorbed in the revised action.

You will experience an expansion and refinement of the senses by this imaginative exercise and eventually achieve vision. But always remember that the ultimate purpose of this exercise is to create in you "the Spirit of Jesus", which is continual forgiveness of sin.

Revision is of greatest importance when the motive is to change oneself, when there is a sincere desire to be something different, when the longing is to awaken the ideal active spirit of forgiveness.

Without imagination, man remains a being of sin. Man either goes forward to imagination or remains imprisoned in his senses. To go forward to imagination is to forgive. Forgiveness is the life of the imagination.

The art of living is the art of forgiving.

Forgiveness is, in fact, experiencing in imagination the revised version of the day, experiencing in imagination what you wish you had experienced in the flesh. Every time one really forgives, that is, every time one relives the event as it should have been lived, one is born again.

"Father, forgive them"

is not the plea that comes once a year but the opportunity that comes every day. The idea of forgiving is a daily possibility, and, if it is sincerely done, it will lift man to higher and higher levels of being.

He will experience a daily Easter, and Easter is the idea of rising transformed. And that should be almost a continuous process.

Freedom and forgiveness are indissolubly linked. Not to forgive is to be at war with ourselves, for we are freed according to our capacity to forgive.

"Forgive, and you shall be forgiven."

Forgive, not merely from a sense of duty or service; forgive because you want to.

> *"Thy ways are ways of pleasantness and all thy paths are peace."*

You must take pleasure in revision. You can forgive others effectively only when you have a sincere desire to identify them with their ideal.

Duty has no momentum. Forgiveness is a matter of deliberately withdrawing attention from the unrevised day and giving it full strength, and joyously, to the revised day.

If a man begins to revise even a little of the vexations and troubles of the day, then he begins to work practically on himself. Every revision is a victory over himself and therefore a victory over his enemy.

> *"A man's foes are those of his own household."*

and his household is his state of mind. He changes his future as he revises his day.

When a man practices the art of forgiveness, of revision, however factual the scene on which sight then rests, he revises it with his imagination and gazes on one never before witnessed.

The magnitude of the change which any act of revision involves makes such change appear wholly improbable to the realist, the unimaginative man; but the radical changes in the fortunes of the Prodigal were all produced by a "change of heart".

The battle man fights is fought out in his own imagination. The man who does not revise the day has lost the vision of that life, into the likeness of which it is the true labor of the "Spirit of Jesus" to transform this life.

> *"All things whatsoever ye would that men should do to you, even so do ye to them: for this is the law."*

Here is the way an artist friend forgave herself and was set free from pain, annoyance and unfriendliness. Knowing that nothing but forgetfulness and forgiveness will bring us to new values, she cast herself upon her imagination and escaped from the prison of her senses.

She writes:

"Thursday, I taught all day in the art school. Only one small thing marred the day. Coming into my afternoon classroom, I discovered the janitor had left all the chairs on top of the desks after cleaning the floor. As I lifted a chair down, it slipped from my grasp and struck me a sharp blow on the instep of my right foot. I immediately examined my thoughts and found that I had criticized the man for not doing his job properly. Since he had lost his helper, I realized he probably felt he had done more than enough and it was an unwanted gift that had bounced and hit me on the foot. Looking down at my foot, I saw both my skin and nylons were intact, so forgot the whole thing.

"That night, after I had been working intensely for about three hours on a drawing, I decided to make myself a cup of coffee. To my utter amazement, I couldn't manage my right foot at all and it was giving out great bumps of pain. I hopped over to a chair and took off my slipper to look at it. The entire foot was a strange purplish pink, swollen out of shape and red hot. I tried walking on it and found that it just flapped. I had no control over it whatsoever. It looked like one of two things: either I had cracked a bone when I dropped the chair on it or something could be dislocated.

"'No use speculating what it is. Better get rid of it right away.' So I became quiet, all ready to melt myself into light. To my complete bewilderment, my imagination refused to cooperate. It just said 'No.' This sort of thing often happens when I am painting. I just started to argue 'Why not?' It just kept saying 'No.' Finally, I gave up and said, 'You know I am in pain. I am trying hard not to be frightened, but you are the boss. What do you want to do?'

The answer:

'Go to bed and review the day's events.'

So I said 'All right. But let me tell you if my foot isn't perfect by tomorrow morning, you have only yourself to blame.'

"After arranging the bed clothes so they didn't touch my foot, I started to review the day. It was slow going as I had difficulty keeping my attention away from my foot. I went through the whole day, saw nothing to add to the chair incident. But when I reached the early evening, I found myself coming face to face with a man who for the past year has made a point of not speaking. The first time this happened, I thought he had grown deaf. I had known him since school days, but we had never done more than say 'hello' and comment on the weather. Mutual friends assured me I had done nothing, that he had said he never liked me and finally decided it was not worthwhile speaking. I had said 'Hi!'

"He hadn't answered. I found that I thought 'Poor guy . . what a horrid state to be in. I shall do something about this ridiculous state of affairs.' So, in my imagination, I stopped right there and re-did the scene. I said 'Hi!' He answered 'Hi!' and smiled. I now thought 'Good old Ex.'s ran the scene over a couple of times and went on to the next incident and finished up the day.

"'Now what . . do we do my foot or the concert?' I had been melting and wrapping up a wonderful present of courage and success for a friend who was to make her debut the following day and I had been looking forward to giving it to her tonight. My imagination sounded a little bit solemn as it said 'Let us do the concert. It will be more fun.' But first couldn't we just take my perfectly good imagination foot out of this physical one before we start?' I pleaded. 'By all means.'

"That done, I had a lovely time at the concert and my friend got a tremendous ovation.

"By now I was very, very sleepy and fell asleep doing my project. The next morning, as I was putting on my slipper, I suddenly had a quick memory picture of withdrawing a discolored and swollen foot from the same slipper. I took my foot out and looked at it. It was perfectly normal in every respect. There was a tiny pink spot on the instep where I remembered I had hit it with the chair.' What a vivid dream that was!' I thought and dressed.

"While waiting for my coffee, I wandered over to my drafting table and saw that all my brushes were lying helter-skelter and unwashed. 'Whatever possessed you to leave your brushes like that?"Don't you remember? It was because of your foot.' So it hadn't been a dream after all, but a beautiful healing."

She had won by the art of revision what she would never have won by force.

> In Heaven, the only Art of Living
> Is Forgetting & Forgiving.
> Especially to the Female.
> ... Blake

We should take our life, not as it appears to be, but from the vision of this artist, from the vision of the world made perfect that is buried under all minds . . buried and waiting for us to revise the day.

> We are led to believe a lie when we see
> with, not through the eye.
> ... Blake

A revision of the day, and what she held to be so stubbornly real was no longer so to her and, like a dream, had quietly faded away.

You can revise the day to please yourself and by experiencing in imagination the revised speech and actions not only modify the trend of your life story but turn all its discords into harmonies. The one who discovers the secret of revision cannot do otherwise than let himself be guided by love. Your effectiveness will increase with practice. Revision is the way by which right can find its appropriate might.

"Resist not evil",

for all passionate conflicts result in an interchange of characteristics.

*"To him that knoweth to do good,
and doeth it not, to him it is sin."*

To know the truth, you must live the truth, and to live the truth, your inner actions must match the actions of your fulfilled desire. Expectancy and desire must become one.

Your outer world is only actualized inner movement. Through ignorance of the law of revision, those who take to warfare are perpetually defeated.

Only concepts that idealize, depict the truth.

Your ideal of man is his truest self. It is because I firmly believe that whatever is most profoundly imaginative is, in reality, most directly practical that I ask you to live imaginatively and to think into, and to personally appropriate the transcendent saying

"Christ in you, the hope of glory."

Don't blame; only resolve. It is not man and the earth at their loveliest, but you practicing the art of revision make paradise. The evidence of this truth can lie only in your own experience of it. Try revising the day.

It is to the pruning shears of revision that we owe our prime fruit.

Chapter 24

Chapter 5 of Awakened Imagination & the Search

The Coin of Heaven

"Does a firm persuasion that a thing is so, make it so?"

And the prophet replied, "All poets believe that it does. And in ages of imagination, this firm persuasion removed mountains: but many are not capable of a firm persuasion of anything."
. . . Blake

"Let every man be fully persuaded in his own mind."

Persuasion is an inner effort of intense attention. To listen attentively as though you heard is to evoke, to activate. By listening, you can hear what you want to hear and persuade those beyond the range of the outer ear.

Speak it inwardly in your imagination only.

Make your inner conversation match your fulfilled desire. What you desire to hear without, you must hear within. Embrace the without within and become one who hears only that which implies the fulfillment of his desire, and all the external happenings in the world will become a bridge leading to the objective realization of your desire.

Your inner speech is perpetually written all around you in happenings. Learn to relate these happenings to your inner speech and you will become self-taught.

By inner speech is meant those mental conversations which you carry on with yourself. They may be inaudible when you are awake because of the noise and distractions of the outer world of becoming, but they are quite audible in deep meditation and dream.

But whether they be audible or inaudible, you are their author and fashion your world in their likeness.

> *"There is a God in heaven [and heaven is within you] that revealeth secrets, and maketh known to the king Nebuchadnezzar what shall be in the latter days. Thy dream, and the visions of thy head upon thy bed, are these."*

Inner speech from premises of fulfilled desire is the way to create an intelligible world for yourself.

Observe your inner speech for it is the cause of future action. Inner speech reveals the state of consciousness from which you view the world. Make your inner speech match your fulfilled desire, for your inner speech is manifested all around you in happenings.

> *"If any man offend not in word, the same is a perfect man and able also to bridle the whole body. Behold, we put bits in the horses' mouths, that they may obey us; and we turn about their whole body. Behold also the ships, which though they be so great, and are driven by fierce winds, yet are they turned about with a very small helm, whithersoever the governor listeth. Even so the tongue is a little member, and boasteth great things. Behold, how great a matter a little fire kindleth!"*

The whole manifested world goes to show us what use we have made of the Word . . Inner Speech.

An uncritical observation of our inner talking will reveal to us the ideas from which we view the world. Inner talking mirrors our imagination, and our imagination mirrors the state with which it is fused.

If the state with which we are fused is the cause of the phenomenon of our life, then we are relieved of the burden of wondering what to do, for we have no alternative but to identify ourselves with our aim, and inasmuch as the state with which we are identified mirrors itself in our inner speech, then to change the state with which we are fused, we must first change our inner talking.

It is our inner conversations which make tomorrow's facts.

*"Put off the former conversation, the old man,
which is corrupt... and be renewed in the spirit
of your mind... put on the new man, which is
created in righteousness."*

Our minds, like our stomachs,
are whetted by change of food.
. . . Quintillian

Stop all of the old mechanical negative inner talking and start a new positive and constructive inner speech from premises of fulfilled desire.

Inner talking is the beginning, the sowing of the seeds of future action. To determine the action, you must consciously initiate and control your inner talking.

Construct a sentence which implies the fulfillment of your aim, such as

"I have a large, steady, dependable income, consistent with integrity and mutual benefit", or "I AM happily married", "I AM wanted", "I AM contributing to the good of the world", and repeat such a sentence over and over until you are inwardly affected by it.

Our inner speech represents in various ways the world we live in.

"In the beginning was the Word."

That which ye sow ye reap. See yonder
fields! The sesamum was sesamum, the
corn was corn. The Silence and the Darkness
knew! So is a man's fate born.
. . . The Light of Asia

Ends run true to origins.

> Those that go searching for love only
> make manifest their own lovelessness.
> And the loveless never find love, only
> the loving find love, and they never have
> to seek for it.
> ... D. H. Lawrence

Man attracts what he is. The art of life is to sustain the feeling of the wish fulfilled and let things come to you, not to go after them or think they flee away.

Observe your inner talking and remember your aim. Do they match? Does your inner talking match what you would say audibly had you achieved your goal?

The individual's inner speech and actions attract the conditions of his life. Through uncritical self-observation of your inner talking you find where you are in the inner world, and where you are in the inner world is what you are in the outer world. You put on the new man whenever ideals and inner speech match. In this way alone can the new man be born.

Inner talking matures in the dark. From the dark it issues into the light. The right inner speech is the speech that would be yours were you to realize your ideal.

In other words, it is the speech of fulfilled desire.

"I AM that."

> There are two gifts which God has bestowed upon
> man alone, and on no other mortal creature. These
> two are mind and speech; and the gift of mind and
> speech is equivalent to that of immortality. If a man
> uses these two gifts rightly, he will differ in nothing
> from the immortals... and when he quits the body,
> mind and speech will be his guides, and by them he
> will be brought into the troop of the gods and the souls
> that have attained to bliss.

... Hermetica, Walter Scott's translation

The circumstances and conditions of life are out pictured inner talking, solidified sound.

Inner speech calls events into existence.

In every event, is the creative sound that is its life and being. All that a man believes and consents to as true reveals itself in his inner speech. It is his Word, his life.

Try to notice what you are saying in yourself at this moment, to what thoughts and feelings you are consenting. They will be perfectly woven into your tapestry of life.

To change your life, you must change your inner talking, for "life", said Hermes, "is the union of Word and Mind".

When imagination matches your inner speech to fulfilled desire, there will then be a straight path in yourself from within out, and the without will instantly reflect the within for you, and you will know reality is only actualized inner talking.

*"Receive with meekness the inborn Word
which is able to save your souls."*

Every stage of man's progress is made by the conscious exercise of his imagination matching his inner speech to his fulfilled desire. Because man does not perfectly match them, the results are uncertain, while they might be perfectly certain.

Persistent assumption of the wish fulfilled is the means of fulfilling the intention.

As we control our inner talking, matching it to our fulfilled desires, we can lay aside all other processes. Then we simply act by clear imagination and intention. We imagine the wish fulfilled and carry on mental conversations from that premise.

Through controlled inner talking from premises of fulfilled desire, seeming miracles are performed.

The future becomes the present and reveals itself in our inner speech. To be held by the inner speech of fulfilled desire is to be safely anchored in life.

Our lives may seem to be broken by events, but they are never broken so long as we retain the inner speech of fulfilled desire. All happiness depends on the active voluntary use of imagination to construct and inwardly affirm that we are what we want to be.

We match ourselves to our ideals by constantly remembering our aim and identifying ourselves with it. We fuse with our aims by frequently occupying the feeling of our wish fulfilled. It is the frequency, the habitual occupancy, that is the secret of success. The oftener we do it, the more natural it is. Fancy assembles. Continuous imagination fuses.

It is possible to resolve every situation by the proper use of imagination. Our task is to get the right sentence, the one which implies that our desire is realized, and fire the imagination with it. All this is intimately connected with the mystery of

"the still small voice".

Inner talking reveals the activities of imagination, activities which are the causes of the circumstances of life. As a rule, man is totally unaware of his inner talking and therefore sees himself not as the cause but the victim of circumstance.

To consciously create circumstance, man must consciously direct his inner speech, matching "the still small voice" to his fulfilled desires.

"He calls things not seen as though they were."

Right inner speech is essential. It is the greatest of the arts. It is the way out of limitation into freedom. Ignorance of this art has made the world a battlefield and penitentiary where blood and sweat alone are expected, when it should be a place of marveling and wondering.

Right inner talking is the first step to becoming what you want to be.

> Speech is an image of mind, and mind
> is an image of God.
> ... Hermetica, Scott translation

On the morning of April 12, 1953, my wife was awakened by the sound of a great voice of authority speaking within her and saying, "You must stop spending your thoughts, time, and money. Everything in life must be an investment."

To spend is to waste, to squander, to layout without return.

To invest is to layout for a purpose from which a profit is expected.

This revelation of my wife is about the importance of the moment. It is about the transformation of the moment. What we desire does not lie in the future but in ourselves at this very moment.

At any moment in our lives, we are faced with an infinite choice:

"what we are and what we want to be".

And what we want to be is already existent, but to realize it we must match our inner speech and actions to it.

> *"If two of you shall agree on earth as touching anything that they shall ask, it shall be done for them of My Father which is in heaven."*

It is only what is done now that counts. The present moment does not recede into the past. It advances into the future to confront us, spent or invested.

Thought is the coin of heaven. Money is its earthly symbol. Every moment must be invested, and our inner talking reveals whether we are spending or investing. Be more interested in what you are inwardly "saying now" than what you "have said" by choosing wisely what you think and what you feel now.

Any time we feel misunderstood, misused, neglected, suspicious, afraid, we are spending our thoughts and wasting our time.

Whenever we assume the feeling of being what we want to be, we are investing.

We cannot abandon the moment to negative inner talking and expect to retain command of life. Before us go the results of all that seemingly is behind.

Not gone is the last moment . . but oncoming.

"My word shall not return unto Me void,
but it shall accomplish that which I please,
and it shall prosper in the thing whereto I sent it."

The circumstances of life are the muffled utterances of the inner talking that made them . . the word made visible.

"The Word", said Hermes,

"is Son, and the Mind is Father of the Word.
They are not separate one from the other;
for life is the union of Word and Mind."

"He willed us forth from Himself
by the Word of Truth."

"Let us be imitators of God as dear children"

and use our inner speech wisely to mold an outer world in harmony with our ideal.

*"The Lord spake by me, and His
Word was in my tongue."*

The mouth of God is the mind of man. Feed God only the best.

*"Whatsoever things are of good report...
think on these things."*

The present moment is always precisely right for an investment, to inwardly speak the right word.

*"The word is very near to you, in your mouth,
and in your heart, that you may do it. See, I
have set before you this day life and good,
death and evil, blessings and cursings. Choose life."*

You choose life and good and blessings by being that which you choose. Like is known to like alone. Make your inner speech bless and give good reports.

Man's ignorance of the future is the result of his ignorance of his inner talking. His inner talking mirrors his imagination, and his imagination is a government in which the opposition never comes into power.

If the reader asks,

*"What if the inner speech remains subjective and is
unable to find an object for its love?"*,

the answer is: it will not remain subjective, for the very simple reason that inner speech is always objectifying itself.

What frustrates and festers and becomes the disease that afflicts humanity is man's ignorance of the art of matching inner words to fulfilled desire. Inner speech mirrors imagination, and imagination is Christ.

Alter your inner speech, and your perceptual world changes.

Whenever inner speech and desire are in conflict, inner speech invariably wins. Because inner speech objectifies itself, it is easy to see that if it matches desire, desire will be objectively realized.

Were this not so, I would say with Blake,

*"Sooner murder an infant in its cradle
than nurse unacted desires."*

But I know from experience,

"The tongue... setteth on fire the course of nature."

Chapter 25

Chapter 6 of Awakened Imagination & the Search

It is Within

> . . . Rivers, Mountains, Cities, Villages,
> All are Human, & when you enter into
> their Bosoms you walk
> In Heavens & Earths, as in your own
> Bosom you bear your Heaven
> And Earth & all you behold; tho' it
> appears Without, it is Within,
> In your Imagination, of which this World
> of Mortality is but a Shadow.
> . . . Blake

The inner world was as real to Blake as the outer land of waking life.

He looked upon his dreams and visions as the realities of the forms of nature. Blake reduced everything to the bedrock of his own consciousness.

"The Kingdom of Heaven is within you."

The Real Man, the Imaginative Man, has invested the outer world with all of its properties. The apparent reality of the outer world which is so hard to dissolve is only proof of the absolute reality of the inner world of his own imagination.

> *"No man can come to me,*
> *except the Father which hath*
> *sent me draw him...*
> *I and My Father are One."*

The world which is described from observation is a manifestation of the mental activity of the observer.

When man discovers that his world is his own mental activity made visible, that no man can come unto him except he draws him, and that there is no one to change but himself, his own imaginative self, his first impulse is to reshape the world in the image of his ideal.

But his ideal is not so easily incarnated. In that moment when he ceases to conform to external discipline, he must impose upon himself a far more rigorous discipline, the self-discipline upon which the realization of his ideal depends.

Imagination is not entirely untrammeled and free to move at will without any rules to constrain it. In fact, the contrary is true. Imagination travels according to habit. Imagination has choice, but it chooses according to habit.

Awake or asleep, man's imagination is constrained to follow certain definite patterns. It is this benumbing influence of habit that man must change; if he does not, his dreams will fade under the paralysis of custom.

Imagination, which is Christ in man, is not subject to the necessity to produce only that which is perfect and good. It exercises its absolute freedom from necessity by endowing the outer physical self with free will to choose to follow good or evil, order or disorder.

"Choose this day whom ye will serve."

But after the choice is made and accepted, so that it forms the individual's habitual consciousness, then imagination manifests its infinite power and wisdom by molding the outer sensuous world of becoming in the image of the habitual inner speech and actions of the individual.

To realize his ideal, man must first change the pattern which his imagination has followed. Habitual thought is indicative of character. The way to change the outer world is to make the inner speech and action match the outer speech and action of fulfilled desire.

Our ideals are waiting to be incarnated, but unless we ourselves match our inner speech and action to the speech and action of fulfilled desire, they are incapable of birth.

Inner speech and action are the channels of God's action. He cannot respond to our prayer unless these paths are offered.

The outer behavior of man is mechanical. It is subject to the compulsion applied to it by the behavior of the inner self, and old habits of the inner self hang on till replaced by new ones.

It is a peculiar property of the second or inner man that he gives to the outer self, something similar to his own reality of being. Any change in the behavior of the inner self will result in corresponding outer changes.

The mystic calls a change of consciousness "death". By death he means, not the destruction of imagination and the state with which it was fused, but the dissolution of their union.

Fusion is union rather than oneness. Thus the conditions to which that union gave being vanish. "I die daily", said Paul to the Corinthians.

Blake said to his friend Crabbe Robinson:

> There is nothing like death. Death is the best thing that can happen in life; but most people die so late and take such an unmerciful time in dying. God knows, their neighbors never see them rise from the dead.

To the outer man of sense, who knows nothing of the inner man of Being, this is sheer nonsense. But Blake made the above quite clear when he wrote in the year before he died:

> William Blake . . one who is very much delighted with being in good company. Born 28 November

1757 in London and has died several times since.

When man has the sense of Christ as his imagination, he sees why Christ must die and rise again from the dead to save man . . why he must detach his imagination from his present state and match it to a higher concept of himself if he would rise above his present limitations and thereby save himself.

Here is a lovely story of a mystical death which was witnessed by a "neighbor".

"Last week", writes the one "who rose from the dead", "a friend offered me her home in the mountains for the Christmas holidays as she thought she might go east. She said that she would let me know this week. We had a very pleasant conversation and I mentioned you and your teaching in connection with a discussion of Dunne's 'Experiment with Time' which she had been reading.

"Her letter arrived Monday. As I picked it up, I had a sudden sense of depression. However, when I read it, she said I could have the house and told me where to get the keys. Instead of being cheerful, I grew still more depressed, so much so I decided there must have been something between the lines which I was getting intuitively. I unfolded the letter and read the first page through and as I turned to the second page, I noticed she had written a postscript on the back of the first sheet. It consisted of an extremely blunt and heavy-handed description of an unlovely trait in my character which I had struggled for years to overcome, and for the past two years I thought I had succeeded. Yet here it was again, described with clinical exactitude.

"I was stunned and desolated. I thought to myself, 'What is this letter trying to tell me? In the first place, she invited me to use her house, as I have been seeing myself in some lovely home during the holidays. In the second place, nothing comes to me except I draw it. And thirdly I have been hearing nothing but good news. So the obvious conclusion is that something in me corresponds to this letter and no matter what it looks like it is good news.

"I reread the letter and as I did so, I asked, 'What is there here for me to see?'

"And then I saw. It started out, 'After our conversation of last week, I feel I can tell you...' and the rest of the page was as studded with 'weres' and 'wases' as currants in a seed cake.

"A great feeling of elation swept over me. It was all in the past. The thing I had labored so long to correct was done. I suddenly realized that my friend was a witness to my resurrection. I whirled around the studio, chanting, 'It's all in the past! It is done. Thank you, it is done!' I gathered all my gratitude up in a big ball of light and shot it straight to you and if you saw a flash of lightning Monday evening shortly after six your time, that was it.

"Now, instead of writing a polite letter because it is the correct thing to do, I can write giving sincere thanks for her frankness and thanking her for the loan of her house. Thank you so much for your teaching, which has made my beloved imagination truly my Savior."

And now, if any man shall say unto her

"Lo, here is Christ, or there",

she will believe it not, for she knows that the Kingdom of God is within her and that she herself must assume full responsibility for the incarnation of her ideal and that nothing but death and resurrection will bring her to it. She has found her Savior, her beloved Imagination, forever expanding in the bosom of God.

There is only one reality, and that is Christ . . Human Imagination, the inheritance and final achievement of the whole of Humanity,

That we... speaking the truth in love,
may grow up into Him in all things,
which is the head, even Christ."

Chapter 26

Chapter 1 of The Law & The Promise

"The Law" Imagining Creates Reality

> "Man is all Imagination.
> God is Man and exists in us and we in Him . .
> The Eternal Body of Man is the Imagination,
> that is, God, Himself"
> . . . Blake

The purpose of the first portion of this book is to show, through actual true stories, how imagining creates reality.

Science progresses by way of hypotheses tentatively tested and afterwards accepted or rejected according to the facts of experience. The claim that imagining creates reality needs no more consideration than is allowed by science. It proves itself in performance.

The world in which we live is a world of imagination.

In fact, life itself is an activity of imagining, "For Blake," wrote Professor Morrison of the University of St. Andrews,

"the world originates in a divine activity identical with what we know ourselves as the activity of imagination;"

his task being

"to open the immortal eyes of man inward into the worlds of thought, into eternity, ever expanding in the bosom of God, the Human Imagination."

Nothing appears or continues in being by a power of its own.

Events happen, because comparatively stable imaginal activities created them, and they continue in being only as long as they receive such support.

"The secret of Imagining,"

writes Douglas Fawcett,

"is the greatest of all problems to the solution of which the mystic aspires. Supreme power, supreme wisdom, supreme delight lie in the far-off solution of this mystery."

When man solves the mystery of imagining, he will have discovered the secret of causation, and that is: Imagining creates reality. Therefore, the man who is aware of what he is imagining knows what he is creating; realizes more and more that the drama of life is imaginal, not physical.

All activity is at bottom imaginal.

An awakened Imagination works with a purpose. It creates and conserves the desirable, and transforms or destroys the undesirable.

Divine imagining and human imagining are not two powers at all, rather one. The valid distinction which exists between the seeming two lies not in the substance with which they operate but in the degree of intensity of the operant power itself.

Acting at high tension, an imaginal act is an immediate objective fact. Keyed low, an imaginal act is realized in a time process. But whether imagination is keyed high or low, it is the

"ultimate, essentially non-objective Reality
from which objects are poured forth
like sudden fancies."

No object is independent of imagining on some level or levels. Everything in the world owes its character to imagination on one of its various levels.

"Objective reality,"

writes Fichte,

"is solely produced through imagination."

Objects seem so independent of our perception of them that we incline to forget that they owe their origin to imagination. The world in which we live is a world of imagination, and man, through his imaginal activities, creates the realities and the circumstances of life; this he does, either knowingly or unknowingly.

Men pay too little attention to this priceless gift, The Human Imagination, and a gift is practically nonexistent unless there is a conscious possession of it and a readiness to use it.

All men possess the power to create reality, but this power sleeps as though dead, when not consciously exercised.

Men live in the very heart of creation, The Human Imagination, yet are no wiser for what takes place therein.

The future will not be fundamentally different from the imaginal activities of man; therefore, the individual who can summon at will whatever imaginal activity he pleases and to whom the visions of his imagination are as real as the forms of nature, is master of his fate.

The future is the imaginal activity of man in its creative march.

Imagining is the creative power not only of the poet, the artist, the actor and orator, but of the scientist, the inventor, the merchant and the artisan.

Its abuse in unrestrained unlovely image making is obvious; but its abuse in undue repression breeds a sterility which robs man of actual wealth of experience.

Imagining novel solutions to ever more complex problems is far more noble than to run from problems. Life is the continual solution of a continuously synthetic problem.

Imagining creates events.

The world, created out of men's imagining, comprises unnumbered warring beliefs; therefore, there can never be a perfectly stable or static state. Today's events are bound to disturb yesterday's established order. Imaginative men and women invariably unsettle a preexisting peace of mind.

Do not bow before the dictate of facts and accept life on the basis of the world without. Assert the supremacy of your Imaginal acts over facts and put all things in subjection to them.

Hold fast to your ideal in your imagination. Nothing can take it from you but your failure to persist in imagining the ideal realized.

Imagine only such states that are of value or promise well.

To attempt to change circumstances before you change your imaginal activity, is to struggle against the very nature of things. There can be no outer change until there is first an imaginal change.

Everything you do, unaccompanied by an imaginal change, is but futile readjustment of surfaces. Imagining the wish fulfilled brings about a union with that state, and during that union you behave in keeping with your imaginal change.

This shows you that an imaginal change will result in a change of behavior. However, your ordinary imaginal alterations as you pass from one state to another are not transformations because each of them is so rapidly succeeded by another in the reverse direction.

But whenever one state grows so stable as to become your constant mood, your habitual attitude, then that habitual state defines your character and is a true transformation.

How do you do it? Self-abandonment!

That is the secret.

You must abandon yourself mentally to your wish fulfilled in your love for that state, and in so doing, live in the new state and no more in the old state.

You can't commit yourself to what you do not love, so the secret of self-commission is faith, plus love. Faith is believing what is unbelievable. Commit yourself to the feeling of the wish fulfilled, in faith, that this act of self-commission, will become a reality. And it must become a reality because imagining creates reality.

Imagination is both conservative and transformative. It is conservative when it builds its world from images supplied by memory and the evidence of the senses.

It is creatively transformative when it imagines things as they ought to be, building its world out of the generous dreams of fancy.

In the procession of images, the ones that take precedence, naturally, are those of the senses. Nevertheless, a present sense impression is only an image. It does not differ in nature from a memory image or the image of a wish. What makes a present sense impression so objectively real is the individual's imagination functioning in it and thinking from it; whereas, in a memory image or a wish, the individual's imagination is not functioning in it and thinking from it, but is functioning out of it and thinking of it.

If you would enter into the image in your imagination, then would you know what it is to be creatively transformative: then would you realize your wish; and then you would be happy.

Every image can be embodied. But unless you, yourself, enter the image and think from it, it is incapable of birth. Therefore, it is the height of folly to expect the wish to be realized by the mere passage of time.

That which requires imaginative occupancy to produce its effect, obviously cannot be effected without such occupancy. You cannot be in one image and not suffer the consequences of not being in another.

Imagination is spiritual sensation. Enter the image of the wish fulfilled, then give it sensory vividness and tones of reality by mentally acting as you would act were it a physical fact.

Now, this is what I mean by spiritual sensation.

Imagine that you are holding a rose in your hand. Smell it. Do you detect the odor of roses? Well, if the rose is not there, why is its fragrance in the air? Through spiritual sensation, that is, through imaginal sight, sound, scent, taste and touch, you can give to the image sensory vividness.

If you do this, all things will conspire to aid your harvesting and upon reflection you will see how subtle were the threads that led to your goal. You could never have devised the means which your imaginal activity employed to fulfill itself.

If you long to escape from your present sense fixation, to transform your present life into a dream of what might well be, you need but imagine that you are already what you want to be and to feel the way you would expect to feel under such circumstances. Like the make-believe of a child who is remaking the world after its own heart, create your world out of pure dreams of fancy.

Mentally enter into your dream; mentally do what you would actually do, were it physically true. You will discover that dreams are realized, not by the rich, but by the imaginative.

Nothing stands between you and the fulfillment of your dreams but facts, and facts are the creations of imagining. If you change your imagining, you will change the facts.

Man and his past are one continuous structure. This structure contains all of the facts which have been conserved and still operate below the threshold of his surface mind. For him it is merely history. For him it seems unalterable, a dead and firmly fixed past. But for itself, it is living, it is part of the living age. He cannot leave behind him the mistakes of the past, for nothing disappears.

Everything that has been is still in existence. The past still exists, and it gives, and still gives, its results. Man must go back in memory, seek for and destroy the causes of evil, however far back they lie.

This going into the past and replaying a scene of the past in imagination as it ought to have been played the first time, I call revision, and revision results in repeal.

Changing your life means changing the past. The causes of any present evil are the unrevised scenes of the past. The past and the present form the whole structure of man; they are carrying all of its contents with it. Any alteration of content will result in an alteration in the present and future.

Live nobly, so that mind can store a past well worthy of recall. Should you fail to do so, remember, the first act of correction or cure is always, "revise."

If the past is recreated into the present, so will the revised past be recreated into the present, or else the claim, though your sins are like scarlet, they shall be as white as snow, is a lie. And it is no lie.

The purpose of the story-to-story commentary that follows, is to link up as briefly as possible, the distinct but never disconnected themes of the fourteen chapters into which I have divided the first part of this book.

It will serve, I hope, as a thread of coherent thought that binds the whole, into proof of its claim!

Imagining Creates Reality.

To make such a claim is easily done. To prove it in the experience of others is far sterner.

To stir you to use the

"Law"

constructively in your own life, that is the aim of this book.

Chapter 27

Chapter 4 of The Law & The Promise

There is no Fiction

"The distinction between what is real and what is imaginary is not one that can be finally maintained ... all existing things are,
in an intelligible sense, imaginary."
. . . John S. MacKenzie

There is no fiction.

If an imaginal activity can produce a physical effect, our physical world must be essentially imaginal.

To prove this would require merely that we observe our imaginal activities and watch to see whether or not they produce corresponding external effects. If they do, then we must conclude that there is no fiction.

Today's imaginal drama, fiction, becomes tomorrow's fact.

If we had this wider view of causation, that causation is mental, not physical, that our mental states are causative of physical effects, then we would realize our responsibility as a creator and imagine only the best imaginable.

Fable enacted as a sort of stage-play in the mind is what causes the physical facts of life.

Man believes that reality resides in the solid objects he sees around him, that it is in this world, that the drama of life originates, that events spring suddenly into existence, created moment by moment out of antecedent physical facts.

But causation does not lie in the external world of facts.

The Very Best of Neville - Chapter 27 - There is no Fiction

The drama of life originates in the imagination of man. The real act of becoming takes place within man's imagination and not without.

The following stories could define "causation" as the assemblage of mental states, which occurring, creates that which the assemblage implies.

The foreword from Walter Lord's

"A Night To Remember"

illustrates my claim,

"Imagining Creates Reality."

"In 1898 a struggling author, named Morgan Robertson, concocted a novel about a fabulous Atlantic liner, far larger than any that had ever been built. Robertson loaded his ship with rich and complacent people and then wrecked it one cold April night on an iceberg. This somehow showed the futility of everything, and in fact, the book was called 'FUTILITY' when it appeared that year, published by the firm of M. F. Mansfield.

"Fourteen years later a British shipping company, named the White Star Line, built a steamer remarkably like the one in Robertson's novel. The new liner was 66,000 tons displacement; Robertson's was 70,000 tons.

"The real ship was 882.5 feet long; the fictional one was 800 feet. Both could carry about 3,000 people, and both had enough lifeboats for only a fraction of this number. But, then this didn't seem to matter because both were labeled 'unshakable!' "

On April 19, 1912, the real ship left Southampton on her maiden voyage to New York.

Her cargo included a priceless copy of the Rubaiyat of Omar Khayyam and a list of passengers collectively worth

$250 million dollars. On her way over she, too, struck an iceberg and went down on a cold April night.

"Robertson called his ship the Titan; the White Star Line called its ship the Titanic."

Had Morgan Robertson known that Imagining Creates Reality, that today's fiction is tomorrow's fact, would he have written the novel Futility?

"In the moment of the tragic catastrophe," writes Schopenhauer, "the conviction becomes more distinct to us than ever, that life is a bad dream from which we have to awake."

And the bad dream is caused by the imaginal activity of sleeping humanity.

Imaginal activities may be remote from their manifestation, and unobserved events are only appearance. Causation as seen in this tragedy is elsewhere in space-time.

Far off from the scene of action, invisible to all, was Robertson's imaginal activity, like a scientist in a control-room directing his guided missile through Space-Time.

> Who paints a picture, writes a play or book
> Which others read while he's asleep in bed
> O' the other side of the world . . when they o'erlook
>
> His page the sleeper might as well be dead;
> What knows he of his distant unfelt life?
>
> What knows he of the thoughts his thoughts are raising,
>
> The life his life is giving, or the strife
> Concerning him . . some cavilling, some praising?
>
> Yet which is most alive, he who's asleep
> Or his quick spirit in some other place,
> Or score of other places, that doth keep
> Attention fixed and sleep from others chase?

> Which is the "he" . . the "he" that sleeps, or "he"
> That his own "he" can neither feel nor see?
> . . . Samuel Butler

Imaginative writers communicate, not their vision of the world, but their attitudes which result in their vision.

Just a short while before Katherine Mansfield died, she said to her friend Orage:

"There are in life as many aspects as attitudes toward it; and aspects change with attitudes. . Could we change our attitude, we should not only see life differently, but life itself would come to be different. Life would undergo a change of appearance, because we ourselves had undergone a change in attitude . . Perception of a new pattern, is what I call a creative attitude towards life."

"Prophets," wrote Blake," in the modern sense of the word, have never existed. Jonah was no prophet in the modern sense, for his prophesy of Nineveh failed.

Every honest man is a prophet; he utters his opinion both of private & public matters. Thus: If you go on So, the result is So. He never says, such a thing shall happen, let you do what you will.

A Prophet is a Seer, not an "Arbitrary Dictator."

The function of the Prophet is not to tell us what is inevitable, but to tell us what can be built up out of persistent imaginal activities.

The future is determined by the imaginal activities of humanity, activities in their creative march, activities which can be seen in

"Your dreams and the visions of your head as you lay in bed."

"Would that all the Lord's people were prophets"

the true sense of the word, like this dancer, who now, from the summit of his realized ideal, sights yet higher peaks that are to be scaled.

After you have read this story you will understand why he is so confident that he can predetermine any materialistic future he desires and why he is equally sure that others give reality to what were otherwise a mere figment of his imagination, that there exists and can exist, nothing outside imagining on some level or other.

Nothing continues in being, save what imagining supports.

> "The mind can make Substance,
> and people planets of its own,
> with beings brighter than have been,
> and give a breath to forms
> which can outlive all flesh . . ."
> . . . Lord Byron

"As my story begins at the age of nineteen I was a mildly successful dancing teacher and continued in this static state for almost five years. At the end of this time I met a young lady who talked me into attending your lectures. My thought, upon hearing you say 'Imagining creates reality,' was that the entire idea was ridiculous. However, I decided to accept your challenge and disprove your thesis.

"I bought your book 'Out of This World' and read it many times. Still unconvinced I set myself a rather ambitious goal. My present position was as an instructor with the Arthur Murray Dance Studio and my goal was to own a franchise and be boss of an Arthur Murray studio myself!

"This seemed the most unlikely thing in the world as franchises were extremely difficult to secure, but on top of this fact, I was completely without the necessary funds to begin such an operation.

"Nevertheless. I assumed the feeling of my wish fulfilled as night after night, in my imagination, I went to sleep managing my own studio. Three weeks later a friend called me from Reno, Nevada. He had the Murray Studio there and said it was too much for him to cope with alone. He offered me a partnership and I was delighted; so delighted, in fact, that I hastened to Reno on borrowed money and promptly forgot all about you and your story of Imagination!

"My partner and I worked hard and were very successful, but after a year I was still not satisfied, I wanted more. I began thinking of ways and means to get another studio. All my efforts failed.

"One night as I retired, I was restless and decided to read. As I looked through my collection of books I noticed your slender volume, 'Out of This World.' I thought of the 'silly nonsense' I had gone through one year ago before getting my own studio. GETTING MY OWN STUDIO! The words in my mind electrified me!

"I reread the book that night and later, in my imagination, I heard my superior praise the good job we had done in Reno and suggest we acquire a second studio as he had a second location ready for us if we desired to expand.

"I reenacted this imaginal scene nightly without fail. Three weeks from the first night of my imaginal drama, it materialized, almost word for word. My partner accepted the new studio in Bakersfield and I had the Reno Studio alone. Now I was convinced of the truth of your teaching and never again will I forget.

"Now I wanted to share this wonderful knowledge, of imaginal power with my staff. I tried to tell them of the marvels they could accomplish, but I was unable to reach many although one fantastic incident resulted from my efforts to tell this story.

"A young teacher told me he believed my story but said it would have probably happened anyway in time. He insisted the entire theory was nonsense but stated that if I could tell him something of an incredible nature that would actually happen and which he could witness, then he would believe. I accepted his challenge and conceived a truly fantastic test.

"The Reno Studio is the most insignificant in the entire Murray system because of the small population count in the city itself. There are over three hundred Murray Studios in the country with much larger populations, therefore providing greater possibilities to draw from. So, my test was this. I told the teacher that within the next three months, at the time of a national dance convention, the little Reno Studio would be the foremost topic of conversation at that convention.

"He calmly stated this was quite impossible.

"That night when I retired, I felt myself standing before a tremendous audience. I was speaking on 'Creative Imagining' and felt the nervousness of being before such a vast audience; but I also felt the wonderful sensation of audience acceptance.

"I heard the roar of applause and as I left the stage, I saw Mr. Murray, himself come forward and shake my hand. I reenacted this entire drama night after night. It began to take on the 'tones of reality' and I knew I had done it again!

"My imaginal drama materialized down to the last detail.

"My little Reno Studio was the 'talk' of the convention and I did appear on that stage just as I had done in my imagination. But even after this unbelievable but actual happening, the young teacher who threw me the challenge remained unconvinced. He said it had all happened too naturally! And he was sure it would have happened anyway!

"I did not mind his attitude because his challenge had given me another opportunity to prove, at least to myself, that Imagining does Create Reality.

"From that time on, I continued with my ambition to own the 'largest Arthur Murray Dance Studio in the world!' Night after night, in my imagination, I heard myself accepting a studio franchise for a great city. Within three weeks Mr. Murray called me and offered a studio in a city of one and a half million people!

"It is now my goal to make my studio the greatest and biggest in the entire system. And, of course, 'I know it will be done .. through my Imagination'!" .. E.O.L., Jr.

"Imagining," writes Douglas Fawcett,

"may be hard to grasp, being 'quicksilver-like'
it vanishes into each of its metamorphoses
and thereby displays its transformative magic."

We must look beyond the physical fact for the imagining which has caused it.

For one year E.O.L., Jr. lost himself in his metamorphosis but fortunately he remembered "the silly nonsense" he had gone through before getting his own studio .. and reread the book.

Imaginal acts on the human level need a certain interval of time to develop but imaginal acts, whether committed to print or locked in the bosom of a hermit, will realize themselves in time.

Test yourself, if only out of curiosity.
You will discover the

"Prophet"

is your own imagining and you will know

"there is no fiction."

"We should never be certain that it was not some woman treading in the wine-press who began that subtle change in men's mind ..

or that the passion, because of which so many countries were given to the sword, did not begin in the mind of some shepherd boy, lighting up his eyes for a moment before it ran upon its way."
... William Butler Yeats

There is no fiction. Imagining fulfills itself, in what our lives become.

> "And now I have told you before it takes place,
> so that when it does take place, you may believe."

The Greeks were right:

"The Gods have come down to us in the likeness of men!"

But they have fallen asleep and do not realize the might they wield by their imaginal activities.

> "Real are the dreams of Gods, and smoothly pass
> Their pleasure in a long immortal dream."

E.B., an author, is fully aware that "today's fiction can become tomorrow's fact."

In this letter, she writes:

"One Spring, I completed a novelette, sold it and forgot it. Not until many long months later did I sit down and nervously compare some 'facts' in my fiction with some 'facts' in my life! Please read a brief outline of my created story. Then compare it with my personal experience.

"The heroine of my story took a vacation trip to Vermont. To the small city of Stowe, Vermont, to be exact. When she reached her destination she was faced with such unpleasant behavior on the part of her companion that she either had to continue her lifetime pattern of allowing another's selfish demand dominate her or to break that pattern and leave.

"She broke it and returned to New York. When she returned (and the story continues) events took shape in a proposal of marriage which she happily accepted.

"For my part of this tale . . as small events evolved . . I began to remember the dictates of my own pen and in significant relationship. This is what happened to me! I received an invitation from a friend offering me a vacation at her summer place in Vermont. I accepted and was not startled, at first, when I learned her 'summer place' was in the city of Stowe. When I arrived, I found my hostess in such a highly nervous state I realized I was faced with either a wretched summer or the choice of 'walking out' on her.

"Never before in my life had I been strong enough to ignore what I thought were the claims of duty and friendship, but this time I did and without ceremony returned to New York. A few days after I returned to my home, I, too, received a proposal of marriage. But at this point, fact and fiction parted. I refused the offer!

"I know, Neville, there is no such thing as fiction." . . E.B.

"Forgetful is green earth, the gods alone remember everlastingly by their great memories the gods are known."

Ends run true to their imaginal origins . . we reap the fruit of forgotten blossom-time. In life, the events do not come up always where we have strewn the seed; so that we may not recognize our own harvest.

Events are the emergence of a hidden imaginal activity. Man is free to imagine whatever he desires.

This is why, despite all fatalists and misguided prophets of doom, all awakened men know that they are free.

They know that they are creating reality.

Is there a scriptural passage to support this claim?

Yes:

"And it came to pass, as he interpreted to us, so it was."

W. B. Yeats must have discovered that "there is no fiction" for after describing some of his experiences in the conscious use of imagination, he writes:

"If all who have described events like this have not dreamed, we should rewrite our histories for all men, certainly all imaginative men, must be forever casting forth enchantments, glamours, illusions; and all men, especially tranquil men, who have no powerful egotistic life must be continually passing under their power. Our most elaborate thoughts, elaborate purposes, precise emotions, are often as I think, not really ours, but have on a sudden come up, as it were, out of hell or down out of heaven. . ."

"There is no fiction." Imagine better than the best you know.

Chapter 28

Chapter 14 of The Law & The Promise

The Creative Moment

"The natural man does not receive the gifts of the Spirit of God, for they are folly to him, and he is not able to understand them because they are spiritually discerned."

"There is a Moment in each Day that Satan cannot find, Nor can his Watch Fiends find it; but the Industrious find This Moment & it multiply, & when it once is found It renovates every Moment of the Day if rightly placed."
. . . Blake

Whenever we imagine things as they ought to be, rather than as they seem to be, is "The Moment."

For in that moment the spiritual man's work is done and all the great events of time start forth to mold a world in harmony with that moment's altered pattern.

Satan, Blake writes, is a "Reactor." He never acts; he only reacts. And if our attitude to the happenings of the day is "reactionary" are we not playing Satan's part?

Man is only reacting in his natural or Satan state; he never acts or creates, he only reacts or recreates. One real creative moment, one real feeling of the wish fulfilled, is worth more than the whole natural life of reaction. In such a moment God's work is done.

Once more we may say with Blake,

"God only Acts and Is, in existing beings or Men."

There is an imaginal past and an imaginal future. If, by reacting, the past is recreated into the present . . so . . by acting out our dreams of fancy, can the future be brought into the present.

The Very Best of Neville - Chapter 28 - The Creative Moment

"I feel now the future in the instant."

The spiritual man Acts: for him, anything that he wants to do, he can do and do at once, in his imagination, and his motto is always, "The Moment is Now."

> "Behold, now is the acceptable time; behold,
> now is the day of salvation."

Nothing stands between man and the fulfillment of his dream but facts: And facts are the creations of imagining. If man changes his imagining, he will change the facts.

This story tells of a young woman who found the Moment and, by acting out her dream of fancy, brought the future into the instant, not realizing what she had done until the final scene.

The incident related below must appear to be coincidence to those never exposed to your teaching . . but I know I observed an imaginative act take solid form in, perhaps, four minutes.

I believe you will be interested in reading this account, written down, exactly as it happened, a few minutes after the actual occurrence, yesterday morning.

"I was driving my car east on Sunset Boulevard, in the center lane of traffic, braking slowly to stop for a red signal at a three-way intersection, when my attention was caught by the sight of an elderly lady, dressed all in grey, running across the street in front of my car. Her arm was raised, signaling to the driver of a bus which was beginning to pull away from the curb. She was obviously attempting to cross in front of the bus to delay it. The driver slowed his vehicle and I thought would allow her to enter.

"Instead, as she jumped on to the curb, the bus pulled away leaving her standing just in the act of lowering her arm. She turned and walked swiftly toward a nearby phone booth.

"As my signal changed to green and I put my car in motion, I wished I had been behind the bus and had been able to offer her a ride. Her extreme agitation was obvious even from the distance I was away from her.

"My wish instantly fulfilled itself in a mental drama, and as I drove away, the fancy played itself out in the following scene . . .

". . I opened the car door and a lady dressed in grey stepped in, smilingly relieved and thanking me profusely. She was out of breath from running and said, 'I only have a few blocks to go. I'm meeting friends and I was so afraid they would leave without me when I missed my bus.' I left my imaginary lady out a few blocks farther on and she was delighted to observe her friends still waiting for her. She thanked me again and walked away . . ."

"The entire mental scene was spanned in the time it takes to drive one block at a normal rate of speed. The fancy satisfied my feelings regarding the 'real' incident, and I immediately forgot it. Four blocks farther, I was still in the center lane and again had to stop for a red signal. My attention at this time was turned inward on something I have now forgotten, when suddenly someone tapped on the closed window of my car and I looked up to see a lovely-appearing elderly lady with grey hair, dressed all in grey.

"Smiling, she asked if she might ride a few blocks with me as she had missed her bus. She was out of breath, as though from running, and I was so stunned by her sudden appearance in the middle of a busy street at my window that for a moment I could only react physically, and without answering, leaned over and opened my car door. She got in and said, 'It's so annoying to rush so and then miss a bus. I wouldn't have imposed on you like this, but I'm supposed to meet some friends a few blocks down the street and if I had to walk now, I would miss them.' Six blocks farther on, she exclaimed, 'Oh, good! They're still waiting for me.' I let her out and she thanked me again and walked away.

"I'm afraid I drove to my own destination by automatic reflex, for I had fully recognized that I had just observed a waking dream take form in physical action. I recognized what was happening while it was happening. As soon as I could, I wrote down each part of the incident and found a startling consistency between the 'waking dream' and the subsequent 'reality.'

"Both women were elderly, gracious in manner, dressed all in grey, and out of breath from hurrying to catch a bus and missing it. Both wished to meet friends (who for some reason could not wait for them much longer) and both left my car within the space of a few blocks after successfully completing their contact with their friends.

"I am amazed, confounded and elated! If there is no such thing as coincidence or accident . . then I witnessed imagination become 'reality' almost instantaneously." . . . J.R.B.

"There is a Moment in each Day that Satan cannot find. Nor can his Watch Fiends find it, but the Industrious find This Moment & it multiply, & when it once is found It renovates every Moment of the Day if rightly placed."
. . . Blake

"From the first time I read your 'Search' I have longed to experience a vision. Since you have told us of the 'Promise' this desire has been intensified.

"I want to tell you of my vision which was a glorious answer to my prayer; but I am sure I would not have had this experience were it not for something that occurred two weeks ago.

"It was necessary for me to park my car some distance from the University Building where I was scheduled to conduct my class. As I left my car I was conscious of the stillness about me. The street was completely deserted; no one was in sight.

"Suddenly I heard a most frightful cursing voice. I looked toward the sound and saw a man brandishing a cane, yelling, between vile words, 'I'll kill you. I'll kill you.' I continued on as he approached me, for at that moment I thought 'Now I can test what I have professed to believe; if I do believe we are one, The Father, this derelict and I, no harm can come to me. At that moment I had no fear. Instead of seeing a man coming toward me, I felt a light. He stopped yelling, dropped his cane and walked quietly as we passed with less than a foot between us.

"Having tested my faith at that moment, everything about me had seemed more alive than before . . flowers brighter and trees greener. I have had a sense of peace and the 'oneness' of life I had not known before.

"Last Friday I drove to our country home . . nothing was unusual about the day or evening. I worked on a manuscript and not being tired did not try to fall off to sleep until around two the following morning. Then I turned off the light and drifted into that floating sensation, not asleep but drowsy, as I call it, half awake and half asleep.

"Often, while in this state . . lovely, unknown faces float before me . . but this morning the experience was different. A perfect face of a child came before me in profile . . then it turned and smiled at me. It was glowing with light and seemed to fill my own head with light.

"I was aglow and excited and thought 'this must be the Christos'; but something within me, without sound, said, 'No, this is you.' I feel I will never be the same again and someday I may experience the 'Promise.' " . . G.B.

Our dreams will all be realized from the time that we know that Imagining Creates Reality . . and Act. But Imagination seeks from us something much deeper and more fundamental than creating things: nothing less indeed than the recognition of its own oneness, with God; that what it does is, in reality, God Himself doing it in and through Man who is All Imagination.

www.ingramcontent.com/pod-product-compliance
Lightning Source LLC
Chambersburg PA
CBHW021129300426
44113CB00006B/349